TRANSACTIONS

of the

American Philosophical Society

Held at Philadelphia for Promoting Useful Knowledge

VOLUME 82, Part 5, 1992

An Indoeuropean Classification: A Lexicostatistical Experiment

ISIDORE DYEN
JOSEPH B. KRUSKAL
PAUL BLACK

THE AMERICAN PHILOSOPHICAL SOCIETY
Independence Square, Philadelphia
1992

Acknowledgments

The first author collected the Indoeuropean data, made the required cognation decisions, and made the classification from the matrix of lexicostatistical percentages. He also compared the lexicostatistical and traditional classifications, including the material described in Chapter 5. The second author invented box diagrams and shared in doing the analyses based on them, including most of the material described in Chapter 6. He also did the statistical parts of the monograph, including the material described in Appendix 7, suggested the use of multidimensional scaling, shared his expertise in its use, and prepared camera-ready copy for the publisher. The third author did much of the computing including writing and using the computer programs to create many box diagrams, and shared in doing the analyses based on them, including most of the material described Chapter 6. He also did most of the multidimensional scaling computation and its analysis, including the material in Chapter 7. However, all authors shared in many discussions that led to clarification and development of the ideas. The three authors all shared substantially in writing the monograph.

The authors would like to acknowledge the help of Anton Duffek for his invaluable assistance in the massive preliminary work leading to and following the calculation of the lexicostatistical percentages, and the help of Jayne Miller for her sine qua non contribution of day-to-day work on this project and her indefatigable good humor, good sense, and inexhaustible energy. We would like to express our deep appreciation to those many colleagues and friends who provided so many of the lists we used, for without their contribution this work could not have been undertaken: their names are listed in Appendix 4 and in the index. Finally, we would like to express our appreciation to AT&T Bell Laboratories for their support and aid in many forms.

Library of Congress Catalog
Card Number: 92-70403
International Standard Book Number 0-87169-825-0
US ISSN 0065-9746

TABLE OF CONTENTS

(continued)

1. INTRODUCTION

The lexicostatistical method, now 40 years old, is frequently used to gain information about family trees of languages which are not accessible to study by more traditional methods. The most ambitious attempt of this kind is probably that found in *A Lexicostatistical Classification of the Austronesian Languages* Dyen (1965) which is referred to hereafter as LCAL. Dobson, Kruskal, Sankoff, and Savage (1972) cited 30 published applications of lexicostatistics over a three-year period.

For readers not familiar with the lexicostatistical method, it is described in Appendix 3 without assuming any linguistics background. For readers who want to have their memories refreshed, we list the four phases of the method in the next paragraph. Finally, important points about how the method is used in this monograph are described at the beginning of Chapter 2.

There are four phases in the lexicostatistical method. Phase 1 is collecting the word lists for the various dialects. Phase 2 is making cognate decisions among corresponding words from different lists. This phase is called lexicostatistical comparison. Phase 3 is calculating the lexicostatistical percentages, i.e., calculating the percentage of cognates shared by each pair of lists. Phase 4 is subgrouping the word lists by using the lexicostatistical percentages. This phase is the subgrouping phase of the lexicostatistical method.

By the way, as used in this monograph, *subgrouping*, *classification*, *hierarchical classification*, and *family tree* share one major meaning, though *family tree* refers only to the result while the other phrases can be used to refer both to the result and to the process by which it is found. The lexicostatistical method, like the comparative method so prized by linguists, has at its heart the law of regular phonetic change, sometimes referred to as the regularity of phonetic change or the regularity of sound change. In fact this method is little more than a new application of the comparative method and rests on the same assumptions. It relies, however, on the more plentiful lexical innovations rather than the relatively few innovations available in the traditional use of the comparative method. To deal with the abundance of innovations, it uses principles from statistics. Much as the application of statistics has been a modernizing trend in other sciences, the advent of lexicostatistics is a modernizing innovation in comparative linguistics and should be welcomed as an expansion of the linguistic horizon.

1.1 The Purposes of the Work

The first and major purpose of this work is to validate the lexicostatistical method by presenting the classification it yields for the Indoeuropean family, and comparing that classification with the traditional one. If the classification it yields had differed greatly from the generally accepted one, some would have found that reason enough to challenge the method. The differences, however, appear to be relatively small and subject to reasonable explanations. Consequently this classification can be regarded as a principal confirmation of the validity of the lexicostatistical method.

The lexicostatistical classification is presented, in two different formats, in Figure 1 and Appendix 1. Each of these presentations contains a great deal of supplementary information in addition to the classification itself, and is fully explained in a later section. Appendix 2 contains an alphabetical list of the dialects, groups, and a few abbreviations. When the lexicostatistical method is applied in other contexts, historical evidence of older languages, migrations, conquests, etc. is with few exceptions skimpy or entirely absent. For this reason we have used only word lists from contemporary languages and have deliberately excluded historical information in forming the lexicostatistical classification of the Indoeuropean languages. This restriction is not intrinsic to lexicostatistics.

Prior comparison of a lexicostatistical classification with the traditional one was carried out by Sankoff (1969, unpublished). His comparison was based on a list of more than 1000 meanings available in Buck (1949), where entries are given for 31 Indoeuropean languages and dialects, many of them noncontemporary. Although these results are certainly reassuring as a justification for the use of cognate lexicon in language subgrouping, they are based on a substantially more meanings than the number used in most lexicostatistical applications, including LCAL, and thus do not provide the needed assurance that the typical use of the lexicostatistical method has a sound basis. Furthermore, the greater number of lists treated in the present study gives it the advantage of being more nearly comparable in size with LCAL as an investigation.

The lexicostatistical classification given here and the traditional classification exhibit agreement on a large scale. Since the two classifications were reached independently, their large-scale agreement constitutes a reciprocal confirmation. Furthermore it provides substantial evidence for the validity of the lexicostatistical method and thus of other lexicostatistical classifications such as that given for the Austronesian languages in LCAL. This validation is important because subgrouping the Austronesian languages by traditional methods is not feasible. Furthermore, even if it could be carried out, it is likely to yield only weakly supported results because the number of languages involved is large, many are scantily reported even when the reports are accurate, and very few have written records from earlier periods.

Our aim is thus distinctly different from that of J. Tischler (1973), who sought to study by lexicostatistics the glottochronology of the diversification and separations of the Indoeuropean languages and Hittite, whatever the latter's status. Tischler makes use of the older texts in a number of ancient languages (e.g., Latin, ancient Greek, Sanskrit), a procedure which conforms with his aim.

It is perhaps worthwhile stressing at this point that no attempt has been made to accommodate the cognate decisions or the lexicostatistical percentages to any earlier classification. It is obvious that to do so would undermine the argument offered here for the validity of the lexicostatistical method. At the same time the word lists used have not been offered in evidence. The aim in not presenting them is to save space, and the action is furthermore justified on the grounds that anyone who so desires can test the lexicostatistical percentages offered by comparing word lists for some subset of the languages cited. We believe that the interrelations among the percentages will prove replicable and that the percentages themselves are replicable within a reasonable degree of approximation, given that some differences and even occasional cognation errors (on either side) are allowed for.

It may appear to some that the agreement between the classification here and the generally accepted one can be attributed to capturing the "obvious" aspects of classification. It should be remembered, however, that the widely supported Indoeuropean classification was agreed upon after many decades of intensive research and controversy, based in part on extensive written records reflecting earlier stages of various members of the family, and sometimes even closely ordered stages of the same language. In view of this, a claim that the traditional Indoeuropean classification is "obvious" can hardly be maintained. Furthermore it is now clear that the lexicostatistical classification of other language families such as Austronesian, which offer few written records and for which therefore it is not yet practical to follow the traditional approach of considering only the implications of detailed reconstruction, yields results that can hardly be characterized as obvious.

Although the lexicostatistical classification in this monograph agrees with the traditional classification in most points, there are a few points of difference, which are described in detail in Chapter 5. Since the argument for the validity of the lexicostatistics is based in part on the number and quality of agreements, it is inevitable that there should be an argument against its validity on the basis of the differences. These differences are, however, far from indicating that the method is invalid, because the few differences are all of three types. The first type results from the self-imposed limitation described above to contemporary languages, while the traditional classification makes effective use of ancient written languages. There is just one difference of this type, though it is a striking one.

The second type of difference occurs where the lexicostatistical classification depends on differences of a few points in the lexicostatistical percentages. Unlike some correspondences between phonemes that are so well and repeatedly attested that the inferences drawn from them approach certainty, the lexicostatistical percentages should always be regarded as approximate. The traditional method should, however, perhaps also be regarded as approximative, for if it is viewed in this way, it is less surprising that different scholars can reach different conclusions, sometimes even when dealing with the same set of facts. The use of qualitative determinants usually attributed to the traditional method seems not to guarantee a universally acceptable inference.

The third type of difference between the lexicostatistical and traditional classifications occurs in parts of the family tree about which there is no true consensus based on traditional methods, but rather a majority view opposed by a respected minority view. As everyone knows, disagreements have always existed about certain parts of genetic classifications in which the issue of methodological validity is not raised, since such controversies tend to revolve about the evidence. As the evidence accumulates on one side or the other, a consensus or majority view is expected to adhere to the implications of that evidence. The validity of the lexicostatistical method should therefore not be regarded as dependent on its *exact* reproduction of a majority view reached by other arguments.

The approach to certainty of inferences drawn from the percentages depends on the magnitude of the differences between them and on the agreements of the percentages among themselves and with other relevant indicators in pointing to the same inference. Although the logic behind the use of lexicostatistical percentages is sufficient to validate their use without further ado, the fact that the lexicostatistical classification of the Indoeuropean languages quite closely replicates the traditional classification and differs from it in almost every case only by small margins can only be taken as a successful confrontation with a practical test.

A second purpose of this work is to present a new tool, which we call a box diagram, for examining a hierarchical classification based on a matrix of similarities (or dissimilarities) such as lexicostatistical percentages. Figure 1 is a large box diagram. Such a diagram presents a classification together with the lexicostatistical percentages on which it is based in a unified comprehensive way. This diagram greatly facilitates examination of the percentages, to see how well they match the classification, in whole or in part, and how well they are described by the family tree model (see Section 2.1) as opposed, for example, to models based on diffusion effects such as those which characterize dialectal distributions among other processes.

A third purpose is to illustrate another method, quite different from a hierarchical classification, for describing relationships, This method, called multidimensional scaling, is most useful for just those parts of the family in which the family tree model is violated because of dialectal variation, diffusion, etc. This method is applied to Slavic dialects, to Romance dialects, and to the highest level branches of Indoeuropean.

A fourth purpose is to present some lexicostatistical results which bear on the controversial question of the higher level groups in Indoeuropean. The answers to these questions reached by lexicostatistics do *not* bear on the validity of the lexicostatistics. Rather, to the extent one believes this method has been validated by the results in lower level classification and by other evidence, the results produced by the lexicostatistical method simply provide one more view. The most notable contributions to the higher level groups are as follows: (1) there is clear evidence of a Baltoslavic branch; (2) evidence is lacking for an Italoceltic branch; (3) there is evidence that Romance, Germanic, and Baltoslavic are most closely interrelated among the distinct branches of Indoeuropean, thus suggesting, though the evidence is far from conclusive, that these three divisions form a single separate branch, for which the term Mesoeuropeic is introduced. Whether Celtic can be attached to this group so that it conforms with the Northwestern Indoeuropean group suggested by Meillet (1922) is not indicated by our lexicostatistical data, though there are reasons for believing that such an association is not contraindicated.

As Indoeuropeanists recognize, there are strong indications of much dialectalization at the highest level of Indoeuropean, so that no classification whatever can be expected to provide a good description of the historical reality. These effects agree well with the traditional hypothesis of a highly differentiated, deeply dialectalized Proto-Indoeuropean. Certainly this conclusion would be consistent with the many contradictory classifications for which weak evidence of a traditional nature can be found. While these contradictions provide only a negative kind of evidence for diffusion effects, multidimensional scaling methods such as that of Black (1976) may be able to provide positive evidence.

1.2 Validity and Reliability

It is no minor consideration in the discussion of "validity" that the term is understood in various ways by different scholars, and is not often clearly distinguished from "reliability." It seems fair to regard the validity of a method concerning languages as dependent on the logical relation between the assumptions that the method makes about the way languages behave and how the data are treated in the application of the method; the assumptions must, of course, be reasonable, as in any scientific argument. We believe that the lexicostatistical method meets this requirement without difficulty.

After validity, the next question regarding a method concerns its reliability. Reliability refers to the extent to which the results of the method are replicable. Such replicability may appear, among other possibilities, as (1) interoccasion reliability, the degree to which the results agree when the same investigator applies the method on more than one occasion, or (2) interinvestigator reliability, the degree to which the results of different investigators using the same method agree. If a method is invalid, its reliability is of little interest, since it makes no difference how accurately the wrong thing is being measured.

Substantial questions have been raised about the reliability of the lexicostatistical method, chiefly on the grounds that this method cannot be reliable if glottochronology (i.e., lexicostatistical dating) is not reliable (Bergsland and Vogt 1962.126). Our response has two parts.

First, the asserted connection between the two ways of using lexicostatistics does not hold. Lexicostatistics might be sufficiently accurate for the purpose of subgrouping, as we believe in fact it is, regardless of whether it has the greater accuracy needed for dating. (This position seems to be rather widely held despite the opposition of Bergsland and Vogt [1962] who say: "From the fact that basic vocabulary does *not* 'change at a constant rate' it follows that, in principle, the lexicostatistic method is also unreliable for determining the subgrouping of cognate languages and dialects." It should be observed that their phrase "in principle" could be read as qualifying their opposition.) Second, even though glottochronology based on lexicostatistics is not used in this monograph, it can nevertheless be well defended. The arguments against it have been made at the theoretical level (e.g., Chrétien 1962) and by examinations of data (e.g., Bergsland and Vogt 1962). The theoretical questions have been effectively countered by Dobson, Kruskal, Sankoff, and Savage (1972) and by Dyen (1973a). Furthermore substantial evidence has been adduced to support the internal consistency of glottochronology, most notably by Dyen, James, and Cole (1967) and Kruskal, Dyen, and Black (1971, 1973).

Though not strictly relevant, two widely overlooked facts about glottochronology are worth pointing out here. First, different meanings are subject to replacement of their words at different rates, as demonstrated in detail by Dyen, James, and Cole (1967) and Kruskal, Dyen and Black (1973). Second, as a consequence (see, e.g., Van der Merwe [1966]), lexicostatistical percentage does not decay in the simple manner of radioactivity from a single radioelement, as assumed by Swadesh (1952) and many others, so that the usual glottochronological rule for deducing age from lexicostatistical percentage is not valid. Instead, similarity decays in the manner of radioactivity from a mixture of numerous radioelements, so that a different method must be used to connect age and similarity; see, e.g., Kruskal, Dyen, and Black (1973). Simpler methods than the one shown there are available and known in other fields, but have not yet been published in the linguistic literature.

Another meaning often ascribed to validity becomes relevant when an adequate degree of reliability is established. The "external validity" of a method refers to the degree to which its results agree with the actual facts when these are available. When the actual facts cannot be definitively established, as in the present case, agreement in results between the method under consideration and other methods is usually substituted; if the results agree, they provide an external validation of all the methods compared, whereas if the results disagree, such external validation fails. The main thrust of the present work is to provide external validation by comparing a lexicostatistical classification of Indoeuropean with the traditional classification. In this sense, their high degree of agreement tends to provide a high degree of external validation.

Consider the reliability of the cognate decisions made in phase 2 of lexicostatistics. (See above and/or the index about the four phases of the lexicostatistical method.) The basis for such decisions is ultimately the law of regular phonetic change, referred to here as the law of regular topophonic change (see Section 1.5). Although scholars differ among themselves as to whether certain pairs of words in the list of comparisons are cognate, such instances are exceptional, and scholars largely agree on the cognation or lack of it in such pairs. It is our belief that the differences to be expected among scholars in determining cognates will change the percentages only slightly, so that the overall classification itself is expected to survive such changes with little or no modification. Our cognate decisions were based on adherence to those of relatively conservative scholars.

The authors, individually and collectively, do not subscribe to the view that lexicostatistics provides the only evidence worth considering in subgrouping related languages. Some detractors of the value of lexicostatistics seem to attribute this view indiscriminately to those who accept the validity of lexicostatistical research. We believe that all evidence that bears on a classification should be considered.

Methods that are equally valid can undoubtedly differ and differ markedly in their degrees of reliability. It is not our purpose here to claim that the lexicostatistical method has greater reliability than the traditional method, but merely that it has a satisfactory degree of reliability. That this is so is indicated by the degree to which it agrees with the results obtained by the traditional method, since otherwise the reliability of the traditional method must be challenged or the agreement must be laid to chance, neither of which options appears to be open.

Nevertheless there are differences between the lexicostatistical and traditional classifications, and these differences are important. But when such differences are found, they call for deeper studies and careful reexamination. They may on the one hand result from error, to which lexicostatistics like other linguistic methods is subject, or may on the other hand contain a suggestion or argument for a new view that will ultimately be accepted. When there are competitive inferences, it is time to examine the bases of the competitors carefully; it does not necessarily follow that any competitor was based on a fallacious method, for its error might simply be greater than calculated.

1.3 The Dialectological Language and Genetic Relationship

There are two matters that are inextricably involved in any interpretation of data leading to a genetic classification of languages and that condition certain areas of such a classification, but do not concern the validity of lexicostatistics. They are (1) the criterion for deciding which set of dialects constitute a language, and (2) how creole languages are to be treated. The first matter concerns the definition of a language as contrasted with that of a dialect, and the second concerns the definition of a genetic relationship.

Lexicostatistics subgroups word lists, and hence dialects, since each word list represents a dialect. In genetic classification, however, the goal is to subgroup languages, not dialects, so one of the fundamental problems of dialectology arises, namely, how to decide which set of dialects constitute a single language. The definition of dialectological language we would prefer to use is seldom feasible to apply in practice: two dialects (or idiolects) belong to the same language if they are connected by a chain of pairs of mutually intelligible dialects, without geographical constraints. This definition is close to, but somewhat more rigorous than, Hockett's "L-Complex" (Hockett 1958.324). Although mutual intelligibility has drawbacks as a criterion, there is reason to believe that they are due to insufficient study and experience in its use. As a criterion it has the advantage of referring to the basic function of language, intercommunication.

To assign dialects or word lists to languages, we adopt here the same somewhat arbitrary rule we have used elsewhere (see LCAL.18): two dialects are considered to belong to the same language if their lexicostatistical percentage is above the "language limit," set at 70%, or if they are connected by a chain of dialects where each successive pair in the chain scores above the language limit. We believe that this rule yields results that approximate, in a rough and ready way, the definition of a dialectological language stated above. No instance is known of mutually intelligible dialects scoring below 70%.

Because of the many different usages to which the term "language" is subject, we specify that "language" refers to a "dialectological language" as defined above. The insistence on the dialectological language as the unit of classification in genetic linguistics is based on the grounds (i) that its dialects can hardly be separated into discrete units without arbitrariness, (ii) that dialects belonging to the same language are genetically related by that fact alone, and (iii) that different dialectological languages do not mix as dialects of the same language do. As the same time it seems to be clear that some pairs of what are generally taken to be different languages, such as French and Italian, or German and Dutch, are respectively parts of the same dialectological language because of the existence of transitions between the pairs.

The designation of the dialectological language as the unit of classification has an unexpected consequence. Voegelin and Voegelin suggest the possibility of such consequences in saying (1977.140): "Diverse, but not contradictory classifications are obtainable from literary 'languages,' historical developments, wave theory, and current dialect differentiations which either permit mutual intelligibility or become barriers to communication." The interesting consequence appears when a dialect from a well-marked portion of a well-differentiated language gives rise to a descendant dialect that diverges and becomes a new separate dialectological language. After its metamorphosis into a separate language, does the descendant remain more closely related to the dialect from which it came than to the other dialects of the original language? Or is it now equally related to all dialects of the common original language? We take the latter alternative. This decision plays an important role in the discussion of the history of English (see Sections 5.5 and 5.6 below). As can be seen from this discussion, the criterion for determining which set of dialects constitutes a language can have a major effect on the linguistic implications of the classification.

Nevertheless it should be remembered that the assignment of dialects to languages is not part of lexicostatistics, and that the criterion used here to make such assignments is not part of lexicostatistics. Lexicostatistics subgroups dialects or word lists, not languages. The assignment of dialects to languages has virtually no effect on the classification presented in this monograph: the only direct effect is through the minor notational convention described in Section 4.2. At the same time it should not be forgotten that in lexicostatistics the conceptual basis for every group is the hypothesis that the group and its members represent an earlier language and (some of) its dialects.

We now turn to creole languages. There are two in the lexicostatistical classification: French Creole, represented by two dialects, and Takitaki. The difficulty they offer is that they present percentages of substantial size with languages that we regard as unrelated, as explained below. We regard the apparent cognates as pseudo-cognates, and the associated lexicostatistical percentages as percentages of pseudo-cognates instead of cognates. We place each creole word list in the group that its lexicostatistical percentages indicate, but otherwise such word lists and their percentages are disregarded in the subgrouping process. Thus, the group that Takitaki and English appear to form is displayed, but it is not given the qualifier "genus" (see Section 2.2) that would otherwise be added, and is called simply English. Double asterisks (**) are henceforth used to mark **Takitaki and **French Creole as illustrated here, showing that their percentages are not used in the normal way. (Double asterisks are also used for another similar purpose described later.)

Genetic relationship between languages is based on the historical criterion that the different languages separately continue the same original language, their common proto-language. The continuation of a language through time is dependent on its being transmitted without interruption from native speaker to native speaker. English is a Germanic language because it has been so transmitted without interruption from the speakers of Proto-Germanic to contemporary native speakers of English. Modern Hebrew on the other hand does not in this sense "continue" ancient Hebrew, but is rather an artificial resuscitation of a discontinued language — itself a remarkable and unparalleled achievement — that reached fulfillment at the moment that the first native speaker of modern Hebrew came into existence. Resuscitation is the appropriate word because it seems most likely that the last native speaker of ancient Hebrew and the first native speaker of modern Hebrew would have been mutually intelligible.

**Takitaki was mutually unintelligible with English at the moment that its first native speaker came into existence or else it would have been an English dialect, no matter how aberrant (see Dyen 1973b.78). It was at that moment that **Takitaki was born. It thus came into existence as a new language. It is not a genetic continuation of English or any other language, and is thus not genetically related to English. Consequently also none of its words are truly cognate with any English words. Similar statements can apparently be made regarding **French Creole.

Nevertheless a lexicostatistical percentage of pseudo-cognates can be obtained between creole languages and the languages that contributed to their formation. English made a significant contribution to the pidgin from which **Takitaki arose and thus gave rise to the large percentage of pseudo-cognates that the two languages exhibit. However this percentage, if taken to be based on cognates, misrepresents the true relation between the two languages, much as treating the many borrowings from French into the English list as cognates would misrepresent the genetic relationship between English and French. The occurrence of such pseudo-cognates in large numbers in creole languages may exercise those who fear that the principle that languages do not merge is thereby threatened in its application to ancient languages whose history can only be inferred. There is no evidence for creole languages prior to the post-Columbian colonial period with its extensive multilingual collections of slaves. The argument for this view and its consequences for genetic theory were presented more fully in Dyen (1975).

1.4 The Lexicostatistical Method and the Theoretical Basis of Classification

All evidence claimed to bear on classification consists of innovations under some theory of linguistic change. It is obvious that a classification is a consequence of inferences from innovations that have the same restricted distribution. To the extent that the lexicostatistical method is successful, it selects groups that exhibit significant numbers of such innovations. Given the liability of lexicon to replacement, large differences in percentages that one language exhibits with two or more other languages can reasonably be expected to have resulted at least in part from commonly inherited lexical innovations, with the obvious proviso that undetected loanwords can be excluded as a factor. Although such borrowing cannot be absolutely excluded as a factor, the list of meanings by which the words in a language list are selected favors words that are on the whole not likely to have been borrowed, provided that the language has not been subjected to "intimate" (after Bloomfield) or "prestige-seeking" (after Hockett) borrowing. Even the likely occurrence of intimate borrowings is normally detectable from the abnormal pattern of a list's percentages (see LCAL.25f.; for a fuller discussion of just such effects, see Dyen 1963). These propositions constitute the logical basis for attributing validity to lexicostatistics.

Anyone who actually works on subgrouping a language family having a large membership is soon struck with how difficult it is to proceed beyond the relatively obvious determinations of close relationships that can be regarded as judgments by inspection. Strong phonological arguments such as those which could be based on the effects of the changes formulated as Grimm's and Verner's Laws, which lead inevitably to the recognition of the Germanic subfamily, seem to be quite rare, whereas other nonlexical arguments seem generally to end up in circularity and/or speculation. Lexicostatistics for its part has the advantage of presenting a careful, internally consistent argument which merits challenge with counterevidence, not with the prejudice often accorded the use of statistics in historical linguistics.

1.5 Lexicostatistical Classification and Reconstruction

It is generally accepted as a matter of course that the proto-language of a language family implied by lexicostatistics is the same as the proto-language of that family implied by reconstruction. For reasons explained later in this section, we refer to the proto-language implied by lexicostatistics as the "proto-language of the original list", which is abbreviated as POL, and we refer to the proto-language implied by reconstruction as the "proto-language implied by the phonemic sequences", which is abbreviated as PIPS. Using this terminology and applying the general statement to the particular case of Indoeuropean, we may say it is generally accepted that the Indoeuropean POL is the same as the Indoeuropean PIPS, and in particular that both of these refer to the proto-language at the same stage of development. Nevertheless, it may be worthwhile to demonstrate that these two proto-languages are necessarily the same, though based on different evidence, since their identity constitutes one of the reasons for regarding the lexicostatistical method as a statistical application of the comparative method.

The phonemes of a (reconstructed) proto-language can be inferred with some degree of accuracy due to the regularity of phonetic change. We refer to this regularity as the "law of regular topophonic change." Here the term topophone is used to specify a phoneme, or a transition between phonemes, or a transition between a pause and a phoneme in either order, that is, either as the onset of an initial phoneme or the offset following a final phoneme. The law of regular topophonic change states that in linguistic material directly inherited from one stage of a language to another, the outcome in the later stage from a topophone in the earlier stage depends only on the topophone and its environment of topophones. Different outcomes from the same topophone arise only by virtue of different topophonic environments; different outcomes do not arise from the same topophone in entirely identical topophonic environments. Topophonic environments are considered different if they differ in any way, even though they share some common features.

Since the regular change of transitions, as opposed to phonemes, is less familiar, two examples may be worth noting. One is the history of the /d/ in English "thunder" that originated in the transition within the earlier /nr/. The other is the history of the initial /e/ in Spanish "estar," meaning "to be," that originated from an earlier initial /s/ followed by a consonant. Although the same regularity of change of transitions applies to a transition from a final segmental phoneme to pause, no example is yet known of a phoneme being the outcome of such a transition. Note that there is some resemblance between Hoenigswald's "nil" (1959.419f.) and a transition; there is a difference, however, in the fact that a transition is here regarded as an element of the same order as a phoneme, though different in character.

The outcome from a topophone at one stage is a topophone or a sequence of topophones at a later stage. Let T stand for the earlier-stage topophone and U for its later-stage outcome. Although one T can be associated with several different U's, a given T in a particular (adequately large) environment E can be associated with only one U. Thus the formula for the law of regular topophonic change is

$$f(T,E) = U.$$

Dyen suggested at the 1987 meeting of the Linguistic Society of America that this should be called the Bloomfield formula in honor of Leonard Bloomfield, who made so many contributions toward achieving recognition of linguistics as a science.

Of course, phonetic change is not the only kind of change that affects the words of a language and their phonemes. Words can be replaced or even disappear, or can be affected by nonregular changes of other kinds which affect their phonemes, such as analogical change. One type of replacement is by borrowings from other dialects and other languages. Such borrowings may give the appearance of nonregular topophonic change. Regular topophonic change can be recognized only in directly inherited material where it is unaffected by other factors.

The reconstructed proto-phonemes, i.e., the phonemes of a proto-language, constitute a set of inferences based on the law of regular topophonic change. Adherence to the law in different descendants of the same proto-language produces systematic correspondences between the phonemes of cognates; such cognates are different continuations of the same meaningful phonemic sequences of the proto-language. Application of the comparative method to the meaningful phonemic sequences of related languages discovers those which exhibit systematic correspondences and are thus likely to be continuations of the same original meaningful sequence in the common proto-language and hence cognate. It is customary among comparatists to refer to such likely cognates simply as "cognates" despite the fact that they are inferred and thus subject to error and controversy; in principle they should be distinguished carefully from the theoretical cognates that play so important a role in theoretical treatments of linguistic change. Needless to say, however, there is no confusion among comparatists, who depend on the context of use to distinguish between theoretical and inferred cognates.

The term adumbration is used below to refer to the way in which a reconstruction is related to the historical reality that it approximates. For example, the reconstructed proto-phonemes adumbrate the phonemes of an actual proto-language.

It seems natural to call the actual language associated with the reconstructed proto-phonemes the "proto-language implied by the phonemic sequences." As in Dyen (1969.512f), this is referred to by the acronym PIPS. The reconstructed proto-language reached by studying the combinations of the systematic correspondences between the daughter languages is called the RPIPS ("R" for "reconstructed"). The RPIPS is the proto-language (exclusive of internal reconstruction) commonly referred to by comparatists as the product of reconstruction. The RPIPS adumbrates only a portion of the PIPS; this portion is referred to as the APIPS ("A" for "adumbrated"). In brief, then:

RPIPS adumbrates the APIPS, which is part of the PIPS.

Reconstruction of grammatical elements can be described in the same terms. Grammatical agreements among members of different groups of the highest order provide inferences regarding the grammar of RPIPS, which adumbrates the grammar of APIPS, which is part of the grammar of PIPS.

The word lists used in lexicostatistics can be dealt with under analogous terms. Each of the lists contains a different set of replacements that have affected what was once the same original list (except for any minor dialectal differences) at the end of their last common proto-language. The common proto-language associated with this original list is the actual "proto-language of the original list," referred to as POL. Despite the fact that the word list of the proto-language cannot be reconstructed completely because of the random distribution of replacements, it is our aim to show that this POL is the same as the PIPS, so that in particular the POL of the Indoeuropean lists is the same as the PIPS implied by Indoeuropean reconstruction.

The lists themselves are drawn from nearly all the same languages that provide the material on which the RPIPS is based. Furthermore nearly all the cognate sets in the lists are determined on the basis of the same systematic correspondences that form the basis for the RPIPS. Finally, some of the cognate sets in the lists are in fact included among the cognates sets on which the RPIPS is based. It appears thus inevitable not only that the POL is indistinguishable from the PIPS, but also that the time of the POL is indistinguishable from that of the PIPS. Thus the Proto-Indoeuropean implied by the lists is indistinguishable from that reached by comparative reconstruction.

1.6 Lexicostatistics and the Comparative Method

Lexicostatistics is little more than a statistical application of the comparative method. The comparative method, so prized by linguists, has at its heart the law of regular topophonic change. It is by virtue of this law that the cognate (i.e., commonly inherited) elements of related languages are determined and thus the cognate sets in the word lists of related languages. This law is a firm indication that linguistics, despite the social character of language and its transmission, has an undeniable kinship with the natural sciences. The application of this law to find cognate sets in the word lists makes lexicostatistics a new application of the comparative method.

The task of establishing a group within a language family bears some resemblance to the task of establishing a primary linguistic relationship, in that each task requires a suitable collection of features taken to be cognate. A proposed primary relationship is established by submitting sufficiently many compared features that satisfy the comparative method (i.e., putative cognate elements). Similarly, a proposed group is established by submitting cognate material containing sufficiently many compared features that satisfy the comparative method and provide evidence of privately shared innovations. Although the tasks are similar in requiring suitable collections of cognate features, different kinds of collection are needed.

The two tasks also differ in some important respects. One difference lies in the fact that subgrouping has the advantage of starting with languages whose relationship has already been demonstrated, so that cognate sets can be recognized with greater security. Another difference is that subgrouping has the obligation of estimating the degree of relationship among related languages and thus also of distinguishing to the extent possible what might have been a group of closely related languages from a collection of markedly differentiated dialects of a single language.

Using lexicostatistics to determine a group within a language family is a sharp departure from using the traditional method for the same purpose. The traditional method relies on the relatively small number of determinable innovations, and compels the investigator to draw inferences from their distribution, even though it is recognized that not all determinable unifiable innovations are useful for subgrouping. For example, the same innovation has been known to occur independently in different language traditions. Furthermore, some unifiable innovations have not been successful as group indicators, e.g., the innovations that produced the so-called satem languages. It is thus not unlikely that it is this insistence on determinable innovations, despite their small numbers, that gives rise to the controversial and conflicting subgroupings sometimes reached by the traditional method or, in some instances, forces the abandonment of any attempt at subgrouping. In contrast, the lexicostatistical method depends on the presence of *lexical* innovations to mark a secondary proto-language, even though the innovations themselves are not identified. It is these shared innovations in the word lists of the daughter languages that raise the lexicostatistical percentages of more closely related daughter languages with each other and thus permit the identification of their closer relationship. We venture the conjecture that two different investigators working independently, i.e., collecting their own word lists and making their own cognate decisions, would find far less disagreement in their subgroupings than two investigators working independently by the traditional method.

It should be stressed that the validity of a lexicostatistically proposed group is not dependent on the correctness of every one of the cognations cited in its support. If there are sufficiently many proposed cognations, errors in a few of them do not vitiate the evidence. In this connection, note that even one of the most remote relationships between two dialects in our Indoeuropean data set typically involves over 20 proposed cognations. In addition, when considering remote relationships in lexicostatistics, one is almost always dealing with the relationship between two *groups*, rather than two languages or dialects, and the relationship between the two groups often involves many more than 20 proposed cognations. Furthermore, the reliability of the individual cognate decisions tends to be safeguarded by the fact that they are made among languages or dialects already known to be related and for which the correspondences marking inherited words are for the most part known.

In any case, use of lexicostatistics to subgroup an already established family should be sharply distinguished from the use of lexicostatistics to establish a primary relationship. We do *not* endorse the use of lexicostatistics for the latter purpose, and we adhere to the traditional method of establishing primary relationships. One reason is that the number of putative cognations among the homosemantic pairs which are used in lexicostatistics is small compared to the number of putative cognations available when using the traditional method of establishing a primary relationship. Another reason is that the likelihood of accurately determining a cognation is severely diminished when a primary relationship has not yet been established.

Cognate decisions are made during phase 2 of the lexicostatistical method (i.e., during lexicostatistical comparison) by virtue of the same law of regular topophonic change used in reconstruction. The decision as to the *validity* of lexicostatistics is not affected by the fact that cognate decisions may be made with different degrees of accuracy at different stages of knowledge of the systematic correspondences, for this difference in accuracy affects only the *reliability* of the results. That can be improved as expertise increases and the original approximation is replaced by more accurate cognations.

2. THE DATA AND THE METHOD OF SUBGROUPING

Recall that the lexicostatistical method consists of four phases, which were carried out here in the same manner as they were in LCAL. (See Appendix 3 for an elementary description.) The four phases are considered one by one, and comments are made about how they were implemented. Phase 1 of the lexicostatistical method is to collect the word lists. To make the classification in this monograph, the first author collected many word lists covering the Swadesh set of 200 basic meanings from available sources for many contemporary Indoeuropean speech varieties. The phrase *speech variety* as used in this monograph means the same thing as dialect with one exception. A reference to several dialects often implies or connotes that the dialects belong to the same language or set of related languages, but a reference to several speech varieties carries no such implication or connotation. Of the word lists collected, 84 have been used in the present classification.[1] These lists and their sources are shown in Appendix 4. Each list is referred to by the name of the speech variety from which it is taken. Where several dialects of the same language are used, the name of the list is usually chosen to indicate the dialect, but in a few cases it is chosen to indicate the source of the list instead. The number of Swadesh meanings which are glossed in each list is shown in parentheses following the name of the list.

Phase 2 of the lexicostatistical method is to determine the cognations. For each word list, the 200 entries that gloss the 200 meanings on the Swadesh list were placed on punched cards, one card being used for each meaning. All 200×84 cards were then rearranged so that all forms for a single meaning were assembled together. The comparatist (the first author) determined the cognation among these forms, and indicated his

1. Eleven Slavic lists taken from Fodor (1961) were ultimately excluded because they seemed as a group to have higher percentages within Slavic than Slavic lists from other sources do. Apparently his lists have a tendency to favor cognate Slavic forms as compared to the lists used. Since this favoring could be connected with a bias (no doubt unconscious, if present), only his Lusatian lists are used here, as no other lists for Lusatian had been obtained. It is not clear whether the higher percentages are connected with the finding by Tischler (1973.133) that false entries average 5% in Fodor's lists.

decisions by grouping the cards and inserting special header cards among the groups. For each pair of lists, the cognation of their forms was determined to be positive (cognate), negative (not cognate), or indeterminate (difficult to determine). Where a form was seen to be borrowed, the relationship between source and borrowed forms was of course negative (not cognate). Where the form for a particular list was missing, cognation between the missing form and other forms was treated as an indeterminacy; aside from those for this reason, there were few indeterminacies. Certain complications in the assignment of cognation were handled by supplementary cards, as described in LCAL. The chief complication arises when a single dialect offers two different words for one meaning and these words are members of different cognate sets. This was not common.

Phase 3 is to compute the lexicostatistical percentage for each pair of lists. Carroll and Dyen (1962) present the program used in LCAL. Since there are 84 lists, the percentages fill an 84 × 84 table. This table is presented in Appendix 5. The lexicostatistical percentage or index for any pair of lists is the percentage of meanings for which the corresponding forms are cognate. More precisely, it is the number of meanings with positive cognation divided by the number of meanings with determinate cognation (i.e., positive or negative cognation). The actual calculation of these percentages was programmed and carried out by the third author.

For every one of the 84×83/2 = 3486 pairs of lists, the number of determinate cognations turned out to be at least 154 out of a possible 200. This low number occurred between two lists for which only 177 and 184 meanings from the Swadesh list were glossed. Only six lists had fewer than 188 meanings glossed. If the pairs involving at least one of these lists are excluded, every other pair of lists had at least 175 determinate cognations.

Phase 4 is to subgroup the word lists into a family tree. The method used in this monograph for achieving the classification is complex, but is based on the simple principle that the lexicostatistical percentage indicates the degree of relatedness between two speech varieties (or groups of speech varieties). A description of this method is presented in Section 2.2. Some alternative subgrouping methods were used only for comparison and are described in Section 2.1. It should be emphasized that phase 4 was based entirely on the matrix just described. To assure that the comparison of the present classification with the traditional classification should be a fair test of the lexicostatistical method, no other information was used.

2.1 Methods for Subgrouping and the Family Tree Model

Methods for making classifications and the properties of such methods, have become an entire field in the last 20 years. This field, in which the second author has been active, is called "clustering" or "classification", and is a prime topic of many books as well as several journals and scientific societies.[2] In this field, methods of subgrouping are most often referred to by the phrases *classification*, *hierarchical classification*, and *hierarchical clustering*. (The terminology used in this monograph is discussed very near the beginning of Chapter 1.) The method used here was developed independently by the first author prior to most of these developments. However, the existence of a large technical literature concerned with such methods forces us to deal with certain questions.

First, how does the method of subgrouping used here relate to the many other methods for subgrouping based on a data matrix that are described elsewhere in the field? The method of subgrouping used here can be described as a specialized version of the popular and widely used "pair-group method" of hierarchical classification that is adapted to deal appropriately with lexicostatistical percentages. The pair-group method has three versions, "single linkage," "complete linkage," and "averaging." The "averaging" version is intermediate between the other two versions, and comes in several varieties, of which the two chief ones are "weighted averaging" and "unweighted averaging." For a brief description of the pair-group method and these versions, see Appendix 6. For a more complete discussion, see Sneath and Sokal (1973.216-235). The method of subgrouping used here is intermediate between the "single

---

2. A few of the books devoted to this topic are Anderberg (1973), Hartigan (1975), Sneath and Sokal (1973), and Van Ryzin (1977). Classification is the central focus for the International Federation of Classification Societies, the Classification Society of North America (CSNA), Classification Society, United Kingdom Branch, Gesellschaft für Classification, Société Francophone de Classification, and the Japanese Classification Society, and among the prime topics for several biological societies. Classification is the prime focus for the *Journal of Classification* (sponsored by CSNA and published by Springer-Verlag, New York), and a subject of interest for several biological and statistical journals.

linkage" version and the "weighted averaging" version.

Second, do other methods of hierarchical classification give the same results when applied to the matrix of percentages used here? This tests both the method of subgrouping used in this monograph and how sensitive the results are to the method of subgrouping. If the results are the same for several rather different methods of hierarchical classification, then it may be concluded both that the lexicostatistical classification of this monograph is trustworthy and also that this classification is intrinsic in the matrix of percentages and not an artifact of the method. To carry out this test, three versions of the pair-group method were applied (by using a computer program named HICLUST, see Johnson, 1967) namely, "single linkage," "complete linkage," and "unweighted averaging." Note that this is *not* the averaging version most similar to the subgrouping method used here, but it is the only averaging version available in HICLUST.

A group is called "dichotomous" if it has only two immediate members. A dichotomous group with four ultimate members, say (A B C D), must be made from two smaller groups, such as from (A B) and (C D) or from (A B C) and D, not immediately from A, B, C, and D. A classification is called dichotomous if all its groups are dichotomous, and a method of subgrouping is called dichotomous if it produces only dichotomous classifications. The most widely used pair-group methods, including the three just mentioned, are dichotomous. Most of the exceptions, including the method used here, are associated with some particular field of application. (The reasons for dichotomy and its exceptions are discussed in Appendix 6.) The lexicostatistical classification in this monograph has 16 groups that are not dichotomous, such as Demotic Greek with four immediate members and Mesoeuropeic with three immediate members. A dichotomous classification would have to use two intermediate groups in descending from (A B C D) to A, B, C, and D: for example, it might use (A B) and (C D), or alternatively (A C) and (B D). Therefore a dichotomous classification must inevitably contain groups that are not part of the lexicostatistical classification in this monograph. For this reason, the only differences of interest between a dichotomous classification and the lexicostatistical classification are those where the dichotomous classification fails to identify a group found in the lexicostatistical classification, and not vice versa. The next two paragraphs describe the differences of interest in this sense.

The three indicated versions of the pair-group method were first applied to the matrix of percentages excluding the few lists and groups identified as deviant in Section 2.4. No differences of interest in the sense described above were found in the single linkage version, nor in the averaging version. Only one such difference was found in the complete linkage version, namely, in the Iranian branch the complete linkage version fails to identify the East Iranian group. This high level of agreement with the classifications from the three pair-group methods is striking evidence that the classification in this monograph is not an artifact of the subgrouping method used to produce it.

The three indicated versions of the pair-group method were also applied to the complete matrix of percentages, including lists and percentages identified as deviant in Section 2.4 and excluded from the classification of this monograph. This is an even more severe test. In this case *no* differences of interest in the sense described above were found in the averaging version! Recall that the alternative subgrouping method uses unweighted averaging while the subgrouping method of this monograph uses weighted averaging. One difference of interest was found in the complete linkage version, the same as the one found above regarding the East Iranian group. Two such differences were found in the single linkage version, namely, in the Indoaryan branch the single linkage version fails to to identify the Marathic and Gangetic groups. These two differences can be explicitly traced to the percentages of **Nepali List and **Hindi that are identified as deviant in Section 2.4. This provides further confirmation that the classification in this monograph is not an artifact of the method of subgrouping used here.

It is important to distinguish clearly between a stricter meaning and a looser meaning of the term "family tree." In the stricter meaning, every branching is required to be sharp and clean. This usage conforms to the notion of the family tree model as used by Schleicher(1861) and as interpreted by Bloomfield (1933.311ff.). Dialectalization in a proto-language, also referred to as diffusion effects and commonly accounted for by "wave theory" or the "wave-hypothesis" in accordance with the proposition of J. Schmidt (see Bloomfield, loc. cit.), produces effects which cannot be accounted for by the family tree model. Nevertheless it is common, and we continue the practice, to speak of a "family tree" even though such dialectalizations are known to be present, as in widespread references to "the family tree of the Indoeuropean languages."

Although the *family tree model* is well known, it seems worthwhile to restate the definition in this paragraph because the method of subgrouping used here is based directly on the properties of the model. In effect, the definition merely encapsulates what is meant by saying that every branching should be sharp and clean. The definition is presented in terms of lexicostatistical percentages. It should always be kept in mind that the family tree presented in this monograph, like the traditional one, deviates to some degree from the strict definition. First, however, it is necessary to make an ancillary definition. Two or more speech varieties (or subgroups) are said to be *coordinate in a group* if they both belong to the group but do *not* belong to the same subgroup of the group. For example, within Celtic there are ten pairs of coordinate speech varieties (each consisting of one Irish and one Brythonic speech variety); within Brythonic there are six pairs of coordinate speech varieties and within Breton there are three such pairs. Then the family tree model (as applied to lexicostatistical percentages) has two properties. First, within a group, every pair of coordinate speech varieties is connected by the same lexicostatistical percentage, except of course for the inevitable disturbing effects of random variation. Second, within a group, the percentage between a pair of speech varieties that is more closely related than a coordinate pair is larger than any lexicostatistical percentage between a coordinate pair.[3]

2.2 The Subgrouping Method

This section describes the subgrouping method that was used here. (LCAL contains a few additional details.) The basis for the method is that each lexicostatistical percentage in Appendix 5 is an index of interrelatedness between the associated pair of lists. Described roughly, the subgrouping method starts by placing all the lists in a *pool*. The two most closely related members of the pool are removed from the pool, joined into a temporary entity called a *nucleus*, and placed into the pool as a unit; this step leaves the pool with one less member. This step is then repeated again and again, gradually reducing the number of members in the pool. By a separate step, a nucleus is changed under

3. Although the language of statistics is not used here, it is worth noting that this definition constitutes the so-called structural part of a precise, fully specified statistical model. Furthermore, the stochastic part of the statistical model has been spelled out and used, though not in this monograph.

certain conditions into a *group*, which then belongs to the classification being formed. Thus in general, the pool contains three kinds of members: lists, nuclei, and groups. Sometimes, as is to be expected, one (or both) of the pool members to be joined may be a nucleus or a group instead of a list. As the pool contains fewer and fewer members, those members consist of larger and larger nuclei and groups. Ultimately the pool contains only one member, the group encompassing all the speech varieties in the data set.

Obviously a measure of interrelatedness is needed that applies to all members of the pool, nuclei and groups as well as lists, so that a decision can be reached as to which two members are most closely related. For this purpose, the lexicostatistical percentages are extended to cover nuclei and groups as well as lists. To explain how this extension is made, it is first necessary to introduce an important distinction between two kinds of groups, *open* and *closed*. The extension is made in one way for nuclei and open groups, and in another way for closed groups. The precise rule for designating open and closed groups is part of the subgrouping method and is explained below, but the underlying concept is this: A closed group is well separated from the rest of the lists in the data set, so that there is convincing evidence for a private proto-language, i.e., a proto-language having exactly the group members as its descendants. An open group, on the other hand, is one for which the evidence of a private proto-language is suggestive, but not convincing. An open group might reflect a private proto-language that is not well marked by the percentages, perhaps because its separation occurred too soon after the last preceding separation. Alternatively, however, it might reflect a (presumably well marked) dialect area of a proto-language. A third possibility is that it reflects a proto-language whose descendants (in the data set) include lists that are not included in the group, due to random variation in the percentages.

Whenever the percentage between N, a nucleus or group, and Z, another member of the pool, is to be defined or calculated, for each immediate member of N there is available the percentage it shares with Z. If N is a closed group, the percentage N shares with Z is the *average* of these percentages. If N is an open group or a nucleus, the percentage N shares with Z is the *maximum* of these percentages. In Section 4.5, the member involved in this maximum percentage is cited and called the *proxy member* of N for its relationship with Z.

The *critical percentage* of a pool member at any time is the largest percentage it shares with any other pool member. The *mating percentage* of a nucleus is the percentage used in the joining operation by which the nucleus was created; the mating percentage of a group is the mating percentage of the nucleus that was transformed into it. The *critical difference* of a nucleus or a group is the following difference, which is always positive: (mating percentage) – (critical percentage). The following paragraphs describe the method as a series of steps, a form of description that is widely used in computer science.

Preparation for the subgrouping method: (Calculate starting critical percentages.) For every member of the pool, set its *critical percentage* to the highest percentage it shares with any other pool member.

Step 0 of the subgrouping method: (Is the process finished?) If the pool has two or more members, go to Step 1. Otherwise stop, because the classification is complete.

Step 1 of the subgrouping method: (Join closest two members.) Find the largest critical percentage *P*, and the two pool members, call them X and Y, that share it. Of course, *P* is the critical percentage of both X and Y. (If there are two or more equal largest critical percentages, either may be chosen. The choice does not affect the ultimate classification.) Now X and Y are to be mated. Remove X and Y from the pool, join them to form a nucleus, N = {X,Y}, and place N in the pool as a unit. (The pool now has one less member, since one new member has replaced two old ones.) Set the *mating percentage* of N to be *P*, so that the critical percentage in one step automatically becomes the mating percentage in a subsequent step. (In LCAL, the term "basic percentage" was used instead of "mating percentage.") Set the percentage shared by N with each other pool member Z to be the larger of two percentages: the percentage shared by X and Z, and the percentage shared by Y and Z. Set the critical percentage of N to be the largest of these values. Each of these values is less than *P*, so the critical percentage of N is less than *P*. Set CD = the *critical difference* of the nucleus by

CD = (mating percentage) – (critical percentage).

Since the mating percentage *P* must be larger than the critical percentage, CD must be positive. If CD ≥ 2.5 percentage points, go to Step 2 (which forms a group); otherwise return to Step 0.

Step 2 of the subgrouping method: (Enter a new group.) Enter a new group G in the classification, and replace N in the pool by G. To determine the immediate members of G, start with the immediate members of N, each of which may be a list, a group, or a nucleus. For each member that is a nucleus, substitute the immediate members of it. If any of these are nuclei, do the same with them, and so on, until only lists and groups remain. The final result gives the immediate members of G, which are denoted by $X_1, \cdots, X_K$. Using the same value of CD used above, if CD < 8.0 percentage points, go to Step 3; otherwise go to Step 4.

Step 3 of the subgrouping method: (Set percentages of an open group.) Declare G to be an *open* group. G inherits the percentages of N. (It may be seen that the percentage of G with any other pool member Z is the maximum of the percentages shared by $X_1, \cdots, X_K$ with Z.) Go to Step 0.

Step 4 of the subgrouping method: (Set percentages of a closed group.) Declare G to be a *closed* group. Set the percentage between G and any other pool member Z as the ordinary *average* of the percentages shared by $X_1, \cdots, X_K$ with Z. Go to Step 0.

A finer distinction among groups than "closed" and "open" is useful within the classification, to indicate how well separated each group is. Though not part of the subgrouping method, four *qualifiers* are appended to the group name to indicate the size of the critical difference as shown in Table 1.

Table 1

Qualifier	Closed or Open	Critical Difference between limits shown		Nominal probability
subfamily	closed	9.5%	no upper limit	5%
genus		8%	9.5%	10%
cluster	open	5%	8%	30%
hesion		2.5%	5%	60%

A subfamily and a genus are closed groups; a cluster and a hesion are open groups. For an exact value of the critical difference, or to check the qualifiers, it is possible with a little effort to work out the exact critical difference for any group from Appendix 1, as explained in Section 4.8.

The magnitudes of the percentage point criteria in the table are based partly on experience, but remain arbitrary in the sense that some other magnitudes may ultimately prove more useful. They are also based partly on statistical considerations: each lower limit was chosen so that a test of the two percentages being equal would be significant at the "nominal probability" level shown in the table. However, these choices were made very early in the work underlying this monograph, using oversimplified assumptions. More realistic assessment yields significance levels that are far more stringent. Both the oversimplified assumptions and the more realistic assessment are presented in Appendix 7 for the most important case, namely the 8 percentage point criterion for declaring a group to be closed. The probability of observing a difference of 8 percentage points or more by chance in the absence of any real difference is actually about 1% or less, rather than 10%.

Consider some group, and consider the group at the moment (in Step 2 of the subgrouping method) when the group was entered into the classification. Suppose the significance test were applied to

(smallest percentage between immediate members of group) –
(largest percentage between group and rest of pool),

and the difference was significant. This would strongly indicate that no other pool members belong to the group, and hence would demonstrate it to be well separated. The second term in the critical difference is equal to the second term above, but the first term is *not* the smallest percentage within the group; it is the mating percentage. True, this mating percentage is smaller than any previous mating percentage involved in the formation of this group, but in general there are certainly smaller percentages between two group members. Fortunately, there is a review, done separately and described in Section 2.3, concerning variation of percentages within each group. This review gives assurance that the smallest percentages are not too much smaller than the mating percentage of the group, which helps provide assurance that no other pool members belong in the group.

2.3 Averaging for Closed Groups

An important lexicostatistical principle is that members of a well separated group should have the same relationship to a nonmember, except for random variation. (This principle closely resembles the first property of the family tree model [see Section 2.1], but is weaker because it is applied only to well-separated groups.) The lexicostatistical evidence for a well-separated group is not only the fact that the members share sufficiently high percentages with each other to group them together, but also the fact that their percentages with nonmembers are sufficiently similar. The homogeneous behavior of members of a group is evidence that they originate from a well-defined dialect chain, most likely a distinct language.

In view of the homogeneous behavior in a closed group, the average of the percentages shared by group members with a nonmember presumably represents the degree of relationship with the nonmember better than any individual percentage. The average percentage tends to eliminate the effects of percentages which might reasonably be regarded as accidentally high or low. Thus for a closed group, the percentages shared with a nonmember are averaged, and the further relationships of the group are based on these averaged percentages. The averaging process tends to reduce the superficial closeness of the nearest members of different groups.

However, there are a few cases where a closed group does not exhibit the homogeneous behavior described above. During the process of subgrouping, whenever a closed group is formed on the basis of its internal percentages, the percentages of the members with nonmembers are compared to verify their similarity. In a few cases, the percentages shared with nonmembers may vary too much. If the percentages shared with a single nonmember vary by more than 10 percentage points, the percentages are considered disturbed. Every disturbance found in the present matrix of percentages has been traceable to the percentages of one member being systematically smaller or systematically larger than the corresponding percentages of other members. As explained in Section 2.4, all percentages of the nonconforming member are excluded from the averaging process, and the nonconforming member is marked by a double asterisk (**) in Appendices 1 and 2 and throughout the subsequent text of the monograph. (Although the 10 percentage point rule for exclusion was not mentioned in LCAL.25f., it was observed in making the Austronesian classification given there.) In the present data set, exclusion occurred in six cases, which are all discussed in Section 2.4.

2.4 Some Special Problems: Deflated and Inflated Percentages

In a few cases, the percentages that a single list or all lists in a group share with other lists may be deflated or inflated by special circumstances. Such percentages and the associated list or group are referred to as *deviant*. When lists or groups are discovered to be deviant, the subgrouping method may need to be modified. In the present data set, the following lists and groups were found to be deviant. They are grouped according to the reason for the deviation. (i) The percentages that the two **French Creole lists, **Takitaki, and the six **Albanian lists share with outside lists are *de*flated. (Here, an outside list means a list outside the named group or different from the named list). (ii) The percentages that **Nepali List and **Hindi share with outside lists are *in*flated. (iii) The percentages that **Katharevousa Greek (**Greek K) shares with other Greek lists are *de*flated. The subgrouping method described in Section 2.2 was modified by excluding all deviant percentages when average percentages of groups were being calculated. (The effects of the special treatment can be estimated in two ways. First, several alternative subgrouping methods are applied to the matrix of percentages without giving special treatment to the deviant percentages, and their results are discussed in Section 2.1. Second, theoretically, the classification resulting from the modified subgrouping method is approximately the same as the result of introducing the deviant groups and lists into a classification formed without their use.) To signal the special treatment that certain of their percentages receive, and in order not to forget this treatment during processing, six lists and two groups are each marked by a double asterisk (**) in Appendices 1 and 2 and throughout the subsequent text of the monograph. (Note that **French Creole and **Takitaki are marked in this way also for another reason, namely, they are creole languages.) Furthermore, some other modifications of the subgrouping method were used, which are described later in this section.

Perhaps the most common special problem is deflation of the percentages due to "intimate" borrowing that has been detected (see Section 1.4). (Any borrowing may replace a form in our word lists that is truly cognate, but intimate borrowing is more likely to do so because it is more likely to affect highly stable meanings.) A similar effect appears in the case of creoles when their origin is ignored (see Section 1.3). In our percentages the former is illustrated by **Albanian and the latter by **Takitaki. In both cases, special processes affect the basic vocabulary, by replacing the cognates (or pseudo-cognates, in the case of a creole language), thus acting to deflate the lexicostatistical percentages. Fortunately, the likely occurrence of deflation due to intimate borrowing is normally determinable. First, as with **Albanian, borrowed words may be directly observed. **Albanian is generally regarded to have borrowed quite freely. Second (see LCAL.25f. and Dyen, 1963), one member of a group may tend to have percentages consistently and substantially lower with lists outside the group than other members do. This phenomenon is not clearly illustrated among the Indoeuropean lists, but two creole languages offer a facsimile: **French Creole consistently shows substantially lower percentages with other Indoeuropean lists than French does. (French is chosen for comparison because it is the list with which **French Creole has its highest percentage.) The same comparison holds between the percentages of **Takitaki and those of the list with which it has its highest percentage, namely, English. **Albanian's percentages with other Indoeuropean lists are consistently among the lowest for those lists, and it is not unlikely that intimate borrowing has contributed at least to some degree to deflating the percentages. (A careful examination of Figure 1 reveals these effects clearly for **French Creoles C and D and for **Takitaki and dimly for **Albanian.) A third method appears to be usable but has not yet been employed. Ordinarily (see Kruskal, Dyen, and Black, 1971, 1973) the cognations between two lists tend to occur most frequently among the more stable meanings in the Swadesh list and less often among the relatively less stable meanings, a phenomenon that appears strongly in our cognations even though all the meanings used are extremely stable on an absolute scale. Because intimate borrowing and creolization tend to distort this pattern, examination of the cognation *pattern* provides a possible method for detecting deflation due to intimate borrowing.

A second special problem that can arise is the inflation of percentages due to borrowing that has not been specifically detected, i.e., inflation of percentages because some borrowed words are erroneously judged to be cognate with the source words and with true cognates of the source words. Errors of this kind are only likely to occur between closely related dialects. As described in Section 5.1, **Nepali List and **Hindi appear to have inflated percentages for this reason. Methods like those described in the preceding paragraph are also applicable for detecting such inflated percentages. Note that it is entirely possible for this phenomenon to be discovered by the behavior of the percentages even though the borrowed words are not specifically identified.

A third problem that can occur is rare: distorted percentages due to deliberately archaizing a dialect. **Greek K represents **Katharevousa Greek, an archaizing form of the language that is not in current colloquial use except perhaps by some families of high education. Archaizing artificially removes cognates with closely related colloquial lists, thus deflating the percentages of the archaizing list with the related lists. **Katharevousa has lower percentages with other Greek lists than they have with each other, but about the same with non-Greek lists as the other Greek lists do. Diebold (1964) discusses **Katharevousa in depth in its relation to glottochronological determinations.

Four modifications of the subgrouping method described here were used to deal with the deviant percentages. Modification 1: The deviant percentages were excluded as described in the first paragraph of Section 2.4. Modification 2: A hesion including all of Indoeuropean except for **Albanian was not formed because the **Albanian percentages which would support it are probably deflated. The critical percentage of **Albanian is 13.5, with Baltoslavic. The lowest percentage between two other highest level branches of Indoeuropean is 17.0, between Armenian and Greek. The difference of 3.5 percentage points between 13.5 and 17.0 is large enough to support a hesion excluding **Albanian. Some ten of the two hundred forms in each of the **Albanian lists are, however, clearly borrowed from other Indoeuropean groups, and accordingly are not counted as cognate. Since such relatively heavy detected borrowing contributes to the deflation of **Albanian percentages, the potential hesion is not included in Appendix 1. Modification 3: Brackets are used in "Greek [Subfamily]," for a nonstandard reason. (The standard reason, which involves the language limit of 70%, is explained in Section 4.2.) The brackets are used because the status of Greek as a subfamily depends on the 69.9% average of the deviant percentages between **Katharevousa and the other Greek lists, and deviant percentages are being ignored. Modification 4: Quite apart from the deflation of percentages, since the relationship between English and **Takitaki is only a pseudo-genetic relationship, as described in Section 1.3, English ST and **Takitaki are not strictly regarded as forming a group, so that their apparent group is referred to merely as English without any qualifier.

3. EXPLANATION OF THE BOX DIAGRAM

This section is devoted to explaining the "box diagram" shown in Figure 1. Such a box diagram displays three things: (1) an entire classification, all at once; (2) a matrix of lexicostatistical percentages in a special graphical way; and (3) how well the classification explains the lexicostatistical percentages. This section explains how to read Figure 1, and thereby how to read box diagrams in general.

Figure 1 presents our lexicostatistical classification covering 84 Indoeuropean speech varieties, and the 84 × 84 matrix of lexicostatistical percentages on which it was based. For the purpose of this discussion, the figure should be oriented so that the names of the 84 speech varieties appear down the left-hand side of the diagram, starting with Irish A, Irish B, and Welsh N at the top, and finishing with **Albanian C at the bottom. Next to each name is a horizontal channel belonging to that speech variety and extending all the way across the page.

The body of the diagram contains many boxes (or rectangles) drawn in with heavy black lines. These boxes are the source of the name "box diagram." Each box represents a group, whose name is printed next to the box. For example, in the upper left-hand corner is a tiny box which represents Welsh, while some of the nearby boxes represent respectively Breton, Irish, Brythonic, **French Creole, Franco-Provençal, and Rumanian, as labeled. For lack of space, names are oriented in two different directions. A few of the boxes are labeled with abbreviations, due to lack of space to place the entire name. For example, just beneath the tiny Rumanian box is a large box labeled WR, representing a group called Western Romance. The alphabetical listing of groups and lists in Appendix 2 contains an entry for each abbreviation in its own alphabetical position. To avoid obscuring other information a few boxes are not completely drawn in. For example the Indoaryan and Iranian boxes (lower right) lack parts of their right-hand edges, and the Indoeuropean box lacks large parts of its left-hand edge.

If one looks at a box in Figure 1, it is easy to see which speech varieties are contained in the group corresponding to the box. Simply find those horizontal channels that cross the box, and then trace over to the left side of the diagram and read off the names of the speech varieties. For example, three horizontal channels cross the Breton box near the upper left-hand corner. By tracing over to the left, one can see that the three speech varieties in this group are Breton List, Breton ST, and Breton SE. Nearby is the box for Brythonic, which is crossed by five channels. The Brythonic group contains five speech varieties, namely, three kinds of Breton and two kinds of Welsh. Further down, the box for German contains German ST, Pennsylvania Dutch, Dutch List, Afrikaans, Flemish, and Frisian.

Furthermore, it is easy to read off the hierarchical structure of the classification. For example, the Celtic group contains two subgroups, Irish and Brythonic. This is evident because the seven speech varieties in Celtic are divided into the two which belong to the Irish box and the five that belong to the Brythonic box. Similarly, Brythonic has two subgroups, Welsh and Breton. Romance divides into Rumanian and Western Romance (labeled WR). Western Romance divides into several individual speech varieties (Italian, Ladin, Sardinian N, and Catalan) and several groups (Franco-Provençal, **French Creole, Western Sardinian and Iberian). Reading off the structure of the groups at a higher level, this classification includes a group called Mesoeuropeic. (The right-hand edge of the Mesoeuropeic box is almost entirely missing.) Mesoeuropeic splits into Romance, Germanic, and Baltoslavic, and Baltoslavic splits into Baltic and Slavic.

It is now evident that the box for a subgroup (say Brythonic) is almost always to the left of the box for the group containing it (say Celtic). This property makes it easy to see the family tree on the box diagram, and is merely the geometric realization of the second property of the family tree model (see Section 2.1). Sometimes, however, the boxes overlap, as for example in the case of Sindhic and Indic or in the case of East Iranian and Iranian. In a few cases, the box for a subgroup is completely included within the box for the larger group: for example, the box labeled M (for Marathic) is included within Gangetic. These overlaps and inclusions indicate discrepancies from the family tree model, a matter of some importance that is discussed in Chapter 6.

At the top and bottom of Figure 1 there is a horizontal scale that indicates the range of values of the lexicostatistical percentages. Note that the scale is reversed, so that 100% is at the left end, and 0% at the right end. The tiny letters and numbers in the horizontal channels are placed with reference to this scale. Each one represents the lexicostatistical percentage of the channel's speech variety with one other speech variety. This means that each lexicostatistical percentage is represented twice, once in each of the channels belonging to the two speech varieties. Different symbols generally appear in these two representations, as indicated below. In principle, every value in the 84 × 84 matrix of lexicostatistical percentages can be read off from the tiny letters and numbers with the aid of the scale.

As an illustration, consider the channel for Irish A at the top of the diagram. Each symbol in this channel indicates the lexicostatistical percentage connecting Irish A with some other speech variety. For example, in this channel at about 83% within the Irish box, there is a symbol, the letter I. This letter indicates that the associated speech variety, in this case Irish B, is connected to Irish A by a percentage of about 83 (actually 82.6). Similarly, at about 34% within the Celtic box there are two symbols, the letter W twice, and at 31% and 32% there are three more symbols, the letter B three times. These letters indicate that two Welsh speech varieties and three Breton speech varieties are connected to Irish A by the indicated percentages. Finally between 8% and 20% within the Indoeuropean box there are a great many symbols. In fact there are 77 such symbols, all of which are digits from 2 to 9. These indicate that 77 other speech varieties, all the speech varieties outside of Celtic, are connected to Irish A by percentages between 8 and 20.

Thus each symbol in a channel, besides indicating the lexicostatistical percentage which connects the speech variety for that channel with some other speech variety, also partly identifies the other speech variety involved. For example, in the Celtic channels, the following are used: I for Irish, W for Welsh, B for Breton, 2 for Romance, 3 for Germanic, 4 for Baltoslavic, and so forth.

In this box diagram, a letter is used to identify the other speech variety if it belongs to the same large group as the channel's speech variety, and a digit is used if it belongs to some other large group. The meaning of the digits is the same throughout this box diagram, while the meaning of the letters varies from one large group to another. The digits indicate large groups as shown in Table 2.

The usage of both digits and letters is indicated on the box diagram itself. Following the name of each speech variety is a digit and a letter, for example, 3D in the case of Afrikaans. When percentages involving Afrikaans in some *other* channel are to be indicated, either 3 or D is used. The D is used for other channels within the same large group as Afrikaans, i.e., Germanic, while 3 is used for channels outside of Germanic. The same digit is used for all speech varieties within the

Table 2

1 = Celtic	4 = Baltoslavic	7 = Armenian
2 = Romance	5 = Indoaryan	8 = Iranian
3 = Germanic	6 = Greek	9 = **Albanian.

same large group, as indicated in Table 2. A letter may be used for a single speech variety or it may be used for a few closely related speech varieties. For example, within Germanic, the letters are used as follows:

G = German ST,

P = Pennsylvania Dutch,

D = Dutch List and Afrikaans and Flemish,

F = Frisian,

S = five Scandinavian varieties,

I = Icelandic and Faroese.

All the symbols in the diagram occur in *matched pairs* which have the same percentage value. For example, the percentage connecting German ST and Pennsylvania Dutch is 85.8, and their speech varieties are represented respectively by G and P within Germanic. Therefore in the channel for German ST there is a P at 85.8%, and in the channel for Pennsylvania Dutch there is a G at 85.8%. In other words, the G channel contains a P, and the P channel contains a G, at the same scale value.

The symbols of a matched pair always lie in the same box. Some tiny boxes contain only one matched pair, e.g., Irish, **French Creole, Icelandic, English, Lusatian, and Panjabi. Some small boxes contain only two matched pairs, e.g., Iberian, Czechoslovakian, and Hindic, or only three matched pairs, e.g., Breton, Dutch, and Swedish. At the other extreme are large boxes like Baltoslavic, which contains dozens of matched pairs, Mesoeuropeic which contains hundreds, and Indoeuropean which contains over two thousand.

The upper and lower edges of each box are determined by the speech varieties that belong to the group. To describe how the left and right edges of each box are determined, an ancillary definition is first needed.

A matched pair is said to *belong* to a box if the two speech varieties are coordinate (see Section 2.1) in the group indicated by the box. Each box is made just barely wide enough to contain the matched pairs that belong to it. For example, the six matched pairs that belong to the Brythonic box are those connecting one of the two Welsh speech varieties with one of the three Breton speech varieties. The Brythonic box is therefore just wide enough to mark off the the twelve letters necessary to indicate the six matched pairs. As another example, all three matched pairs of Breton speech varieties belong to the Breton box. Similarly, the matched pairs that belong to the Celtic box are those connecting one of the two Irish speech varieties with one of the five Brythonic speech varieties. The ten pairs are indicated by the 20 letters in the Celtic box.

Among the larger boxes, the Baltoslavic box contains 39 (= 3 × 13) matched pairs, each of which connects one of the Baltic speech varieties with one of the Slavic speech varieties. The Mesoeuropeic box contains the 736 (= 16×15 + 16×16 + 15×16) matched pairs connecting the speech varieties of Romance with those of Germanic and with those of Baltoslavic as well as the speech varieties of Germanic with those of Baltoslavic. The Indoeuropean box contains the over 2000 matched pairs connecting two speech varieties from different groups among the seven highest level groups in this classification, namely, Celtic, Mesoeuropeic, Indoaryan, Greek, Armenian, Iranian, and **Albanian.

In summary, a box diagram is used to display and to compare two things: (1) a classification and (2) a matrix of lexicostatistical percentages. In Figure 1 the classification was derived from the matrix involved, but a box diagram provides a relatively easy way to compare any classification with any matrix of values, even if the classification is not derived from the matrix. The symbols in the channels present all the lexicostatistical percentages in a way which permits easy visual examination of their values. The classification is presented by the boxes in a way which is easy to grasp. Most important, however, the widths of the boxes and their relative position makes it easy to see just how well the classification explains the matrix of lexicostatistical percentages. An examination of Figure 1 from this point of view is presented in Chapter 6.

4. EXPLANATION OF THE OUTLINE CLASSIFICATION

It is necessary to distinguish two different meanings for "step" that are used in this monograph. The method of subgrouping is described in Section 2.2 as consisting of Steps 0, 1, 2, 3, and 4. On the other hand, when the method is used, each use of Step 1 joins two word lists and/or groups together to make a nucleus, which later becomes part or all of a group. Each use of Step 1 is referred to as a joining step or, for compatibility with the terminology in LCAL, a *mating step*. The purpose of the Outline Classification of the Indoeuropean Languages presented in Appendix 1, like the box diagram in Figure 1, is to present the classification reached here, but also especially to present the mating steps by which the classification was derived. It is a way of presenting the conventional language family tree in the form of an outline together with the evidence for that tree. An outline classification of this type was introduced in LCAL. Although a box diagram is useful for many purposes, it does not show how the classification was arrived at from the matrix of lexicostatistical percentages of the diagram.

The method for deriving the classification is described in Section 2.2 where the technical terms "nucleus," "critical percentage," "mating percentage," "critical difference," and others have been introduced and defined. It is advisable to be familiar with the technical terms of Section 2.2, and to examine Appendix 1 as you read this section. Appendix 1 is highly compact, being designed for repeated reference by those interested in the reasoning from the percentages to the classification.

The outline classification is composed of *entries*, one for each list and group in the classification. Each entry consists of two portions:

(1) The initial portion identifies a group or list as the *subject* of the entry.

(2) The final portion shows the steps by which the subject was mated or joined with other groups or lists in forming a larger group. Each of these groups or lists is known as an *adjoined group* or *list*. This portion consists of one or more mating percentages, each followed in parentheses by identification of the adjoined group or list, plus certain other information in certain cases.

Each mating step is represented twice in Appendix 1: that is, it appears in exactly two entries. Specifically, the mating of a pair A and B appears in one entry in which A is the subject and in another entry in which B is the subject. In this respect the outline classification bears a resemblance to double-entry bookkeeping. The way a group or list is cited in the initial portion of an entry is usually the same as that used in parentheses in a final portion, though there is a slight difference in some cases.

There are a number of unavoidable complications in the formulation of entries, chiefly in presenting the way open groups are classified. In order to discuss all the different aspects of an entry, two entries are shown here in an expanded format so as to reveal their structure. It is helpful to consult them while reading the next several pages. In Appendix 1 these two entries appear without unnecessary line breaks so that the first entry occupies only one line and the second only three lines:

1.2.2.3. Breton ST	
	94.9 (1.2.2.2. Breton SE),
	92.9 (1.2.2.1. Breton List).

2. Mesoeuropeic Hesion:	
2.3. Baltoslavic Subfamily	18.6 (3. Indoaryan Cluster: 3.3. Indic Subfamily),
	13.5 (7. **Albanian);
2.1. Romance Subfamily	18.3 (1. Celtic Subfamily);
2.2. Germanic Subfamily	17.1 (4. Greek).

4.1 The Label and its Number String and Qualifiers

Aside from the percentages, each entry makes use of several *labels* like those shown in the first line and elsewhere in each box. A subject or adjoined group or list is presented in the form of a label. A label consists of a *number string* and a *name* to identify a group or list. The number string preceding a name such as "1.2.2.3." is a conventional type of index. It can be thought of as a kind of road map that describes how to get from the highest group, Indoeuropean, down to the group or list being identified. Thus "1.2.2.3." means take the first branch, then at the next group take the second branch, then at the next group take the second branch, and then at the next group take the third branch. The name following the number string in a label is either the name of a list as in "1.2.2.2. Breton ST" or the name of a group as in "1. Celtic Subfamily." Each group name includes one of the four qualifiers introduced in Table 1 in Section 2.2: "subfamily," "genus," "cluster," or "hesion." In some group names, however, the qualifier "subfamily" or "genus" appears in brackets to indicate special treatment that is explained in the following section.

4.2 Bracketed Qualifiers

Although a qualifier always conveys useful information about the group to which it is applied, in some cases its mechanical application results in a peculiarity. A group of lists that would for good reason be considered to belong to the same language might nevertheless satisfy the conditions for being a closed group: that is, a subfamily or genus. No paradox or inconsistency need be involved. Although the normal consequence of dialect gradation or chaining is expected to be an open group (i.e., a cluster or hesion), the appearance of a closed group of dialects within a language could be an artifact resulting from the absence of information about transitional dialects among the lists. Nevertheless, in order to avoid apparent incongruity, the qualifiers "subfamily" and "genus" are enclosed in square brackets in the initial portion when the group consists of dialects of a single language.[4] For this purpose any group whose mating percentage is greater than or equal to the language

4. The following table shows how the 52 groups are divided into the four types, above and below the language limit. (The group consisting of English and **Takitaki is counted here as a subfamily, even though it is not marked as such in Appendix 1 due to the special status of **Takitaki as a creole language. For further information, see Sections 1.3 and 2.4.) The brackets indicate the qualifiers which are bracketed in Appendix 1.

	Above 70%	Below 70%	Total
Subfamily	[22]	12	34
Genus	[1]	0	1
Cluster	3	3	6
Hesion	7	4	11
Total	33	19	52

limit of 70% is treated as belonging to a single language. For the present matrix of percentages this practice yields results that agree quite well with traditional linguistic terminology.

A bracketed qualifier appears only in the initial portion of an entry; elsewhere it is omitted. Unbracketed qualifiers are treated as an integral part of the label and never omitted. For example the label "1.2. Brythonic Subfamily" has this form in all occurrences, whereas the label that appears as "1.1 Irish [Subfamily]" in the initial portion for this group has the form "1.1 Irish" when the label appears elsewhere.

4.3 Arrangement of the Entries

The initial portion of each entry is a subject label that identifies the group or list that is the subject of the entry. The entire classification is conveyed by the subject labels of the entries. In principle even if the entries were arranged in random order, their subject labels would still provide an explicit and correct description of the classification. For ease of reference, however, the entries are arranged in the order of the number string of the subject labels and are indented in a way that also indicates the classification. The numbers are repeated in a column along the left-hand margin.

4.4 Entry Punctuation

The presentation of entries that show the way open groups are joined sometimes results in complicated statements. The colon, comma, semicolon, and period are used in particular ways, though their use here does not differ greatly from their ordinary use. The colon (:) subordinates the following to what precedes. It is used immediately after a "head label" before a "proxy label." These two terms are defined in the following section. The comma (,) and semicolon (;) connect two coordinate (i.e., like) units. The comma connects simple units and the semicolon connects complex units, as described in Section 4.7. A period (.) is used to indicate the end of an entry (in addition to its use within number strings).

4.5 Proxy Members, Proxy Labels, and Head Labels

When a group has been determined, its percentage with each outside (i.e., nonmember) group or list is calculated from the the percentages of its immediate members with the outside group or list (see Section 2.2). If the group is closed, the average of these percentages is used, and the group's further classification depends on these average percentages, which are used just like the percentages of a list. If the group is open, the maximum of these percentages is used. The member exhibiting this highest percentage is called the *proxy member* of the open group for its relationship with the outside group or list. The open group is then said to be represented by the proxy member and its percentage. The label of a proxy member is called a *proxy label* and the label of the open group it represents is called the *head label* when contrasted with the proxy label.

A head label is followed by a colon, which is followed by the proxy label: e.g., in the sequence "3. Indoaryan Cluster: 3.3. Indic Subfamily" from the second box above, "3. Indoaryan Cluster" is the head label and "3.3. Indic Subfamily" is the proxy label. Similarly, in the sequence "2. Mesoeuropeic Hesion: 2.3. Baltoslavic Subfamily" from the same box, "2. Mesoeuropeic Hesion" is the head label and 2.3. Baltoslavic Subfamily" is the proxy label.

It sometimes happens that the proxy member is itself an open group, which is represented by a proxy member, and thus its label can at the same time be a head label with a following proxy label. In principle the sequence of open groups representing open groups continues as long as necessary until a list or closed group is reached. In practice, however, there are only seven such series in Appendix 1 and each involves only two open groups in a row: e.g., the sequence "6. Iranian Cluster: 6.2. East Iranian Hesion: 6.2.2. Persic Subfamily 18.1..." indicates that the Iranian Cluster, an open group, is represented in this case by the East Iranian Hesion, itself also an open group requiring representation that is supplied by the Persic Subfamily, a closed group and the one actually involved in the percentage 18.1.

4.6 The Entry For a List or Closed Group

In the case of an entry whose subject is a list or closed group, the subject is not represented by proxies so it is relatively simple to display the mating percentages and adjoined groups or lists. Each mating percentage is followed by the label of the adjoined group or list in parentheses. A comma is placed after the parenthesis to indicate that another joining or mating step follows. A period is placed after the last parenthesis to indicate the end of the entry. The use of the comma and the period is illustrated in the first box above at the end of the second and third lines.

4.7 The Entry for an Open Group

In the case of an entry whose subject is an open group, the subject is represented by a proxy member in each joining. To indicate the proxy member in the first joining, the subject label is followed by a colon and the first proxy label. This is followed by the mating percentage for the first joining and the label of the adjoined group or list in parentheses. A comma or a semicolon is placed after the parenthesis to indicate that another joining or mating step follows. A period is placed after the parenthesis to indicate the end of the entry.

A comma indicates that in the next joining the subject entry is represented by the same proxy member, while a semicolon indicates that the subject entry is represented by a different proxy member. Following a comma is another mating percentage and the label of the adjoined group or list in parentheses. Following a semicolon is a proxy member for the subject entry and then a mating percentage and the label of the adjoined group in parentheses. Following either of these is again a comma, semicolon, or period.

The use of the comma, semicolon, and period is illustrated in second box above at the ends of the second, third, and fourth lines. The subject of this entry is Mesoeuropeic. It is represented by Baltoslavic in its joinings with Indoaryan and with **Albanian, by Romance in its joining with Celtic, and by Germanic in its joining with Greek. Consider the four joinings indicated in order.

(1) The proxy member for Mesoeuropeic here is Baltoslavic. This joining is with Indoaryan, which is represented by Indic. The two proxies for this joining, Baltoslavic and Indic, share a percentage of 18.6. The comma following this information indicates that the next joining continues to use the same proxy member for Mesoeuropeic.

(2) This joining is with **Albanian. Baltoslavic and **Albanian share a percentage of 13.5. The semicolon following this information indicates that the next joining uses a different proxy member for Mesoeuropeic.

(3) The proxy member for Mesoeuropeic in this joining is Romance, which immediately follows the semicolon. This joining is with Celtic. Romance and Celtic share a percentage of 18.3. The semicolon following this information indicates that the next joining uses a different proxy member for Mesoeuropeic.

(4) The proxy member for Mesoeuropeic in this joining is Germanic,

which immediately follows the semicolon. This joining is with Greek. Germanic and Greek share a percentage of 17.1.

4.8 Finding the Critical Difference From Appendix 1

To determine whether a group is a subfamily, a genus, a cluster, or a hesion, it is necessary to determine its mating percentage and its critical percentage and to take the difference; this difference is called the *critical difference*:

(critical difference) = (mating percentage) − (critical percentage)

and is classified as shown in Table 1 in Section 2.2. The critical percentage of the subject of any entry is the maximum of the percentages appearing in the entry, which in Appendix 1 is always the first percentage shown in the entry. The mating percentage is the minimum of the percentages shown in the entries of its immediate members. The mating percentage of a group is always greater than its critical percentage.

A few examples follow to illustrate the procedure of finding the critical difference of a group and assigning a qualifier to its name. These examples are taken from Appendix 1, but the adjoined groups have been omitted, being represented by three dots.

(1) This example concerns Breton:

1.2.2. Breton [Subfamily] 62.5 ...
  1.2.2.1. Breton List 92.9 ...
  1.2.2.2. Breton SE 94.9 ...

The critical percentage of 1.2.2. Breton [Subfamily] is 62.5 since it is the maximum percentage associated with the entry subject. The minimum of the percentages of the immediate members of the group is the 92.9 of the 1.2.2.1 Breton List, which is thus the mating percentage of the group; consequently the critical difference is 92.9 − 62.5 = 30.4. In accordance with Table 1, Breton is thus a subfamily, a closed group. Since however the mating percentage is above the language limit (70%), "subfamily" is placed in square brackets.

(2) This example concerns Romance:

2.1. Romance Subfamily 23.5 ...
2.1.1. Rumanian [Subfamily] 56.8 ...
2.1.2. Western Romance Subfamily 56.8 ...

The critical percentage of 2.1 Romance Subfamily is 23.5, the (only and therefore) maximum percentage associated with the entry subject. The (only and therefore minimum) percentage of the immediate members of the group is 56.8, which is thus the mating percentage of the group; consequently the critical difference is 56.8 – 23.5 = 33.3. In accordance with Table 1, Romance is thus a subfamily, a closed group. Since the mating percentage is below 70%, the language limit, the term "subfamily" is not placed in square brackets.

(3) This example concerns Iberian:

2.1.2.7. Iberian [Genus] 78.4 ...
2.1.2.7.1. Spanish 86.8 ...
2.1.2.7.2. Portuguese [Subfamily] 86.8 ...

The critical percentage of 2.1.2.7. Iberian [Genus] is 78.4, the (only and therefore) maximum percentage associated with the entry subject. The (only and therefore) minimum percentage of the immediate members of the group is 86.8, which is thus the group's mating percentage. Consequently the critical difference is 86.8 – 78.4 = 8.4. In accordance with Table 1, Iberian is thus a genus, a closed group; it is incidentally the only genus in the entire classification. Since the mating percentage is above 70% and a genus is a closed group, the term "genus" is enclosed in square brackets.

(4) This example concerns Marathic:

3.3.2.1.1. Marathic Cluster: 3.3.2.1.1.2. Gujarati 55.2 ...
3.3.2.1.1.1. Marathi 61.3 ...
3.3.2.1.1.2. Gujarati 61.3 ...

The critical percentage of 3.3.2.1.1. Marathic Cluster is 55.2, the maximum percentage associated with the entry subject; it has this percentage via its proxy member, 3.3.2.1.1.1. Gujarati. The (only and therefore) minimum percentage of its immediate members is 61.3, thus the mating percentage of the group. Consequently the critical difference is 61.3 – 55.2 = 6.1. In accordance with Table 1, Marathic is thus a cluster, an open group, so the question of square brackets does not arise.

(5) This example concerns Mesoeuropeic:

2. Mesoeuropeic Hesion: 2.3. Baltoslavic Subfamily 18.6 ...
    2.1. Romance Subfamily 23.5 ...
    2.2. Germanic Subfamily 23.5 ...
    2.3. Baltoslavic Subfamily 22.2 ...

The critical percentage of 2. Mesoeuropeic Hesion is 18.6 through its proxy member, 2.3. Baltic Subfamily. The minimum percentage of those of its immediate members is 22.2, which is thus the group's mating percentage. Consequently the critical difference is 22.2 − 18.6 = 3.6. In accordance with Table 1, Mesoeuropeic is thus a hesion, an open group, so the question of square brackets does not arise.

5. IMPLICATIONS AND PROBLEMS

Examination of the lexicostatistical classification in Figure 1 and Appendix 1 gives detailed support to the assertion that this classification agrees overwhelmingly with the traditional one. Not only is this true, but the lexicostatistical method contains an intrinsic capability of assessing how reliable individual groups are, which is indicated by the descending degrees of separation indicated in the terms "subfamily, genus, cluster, hesion" (see Table 1 in Section 2.2). Lexicostatistically determined groups judged to be reliable can be accepted as correct with a high degree of confidence.

The only novel aspects or problems in the IE lexicostatistical classification are (1) the nonexistence of an Indoiranian group, (2) the position of Slovenian among the Slavic speech varieties, and the absence of the tripartite division of Slavic languages into eastern, western, and southern groups, (3) the existence of Mesoeuropeic, (4) the position of English in Germanic, and (5) the position of Gujarati within Indoaryan. These points are discussed in order. In addition, the lexicostatistical classification bears on some not entirely settled matters, such as the possible existence of a Baltoslavic group, an Italoceltic group, and a Northwestern Indoeuropean group. It is convenient to discuss Baltoslavic between (2) and (3), and to discuss Italoceltic and Northwestern Indoeuropean together with (3).

5.1 Indoiranian

Perhaps the most notable discrepancy between the lexicostatistical classification and generally accepted hypotheses is its failure to distinguish an Indoiranian group. The difficulty is not on the Iranian side, for the Iranian Cluster has its highest percentage (18.1) with the Indoaryan Cluster. However, the latter group exhibits like percentages with the Mesoeuropeic Hesion (18.6) and the Baltoslavic Subfamily (18.1). An *Indoiranian Hesion would have been establishable if the Indoaryan-Iranian percentage had been at least 21.1 (i.e., 18.6 + 2.5).

The evidence that the Indoaryan and Iranian languages continue a secondary proto-language, Proto-Indoiranian, is evaluated by Meillet (1922.251) as follows: "... Indoiranian offers an entire series of peculiarities of detail which are found nowhere else and which continue from the common period peculiar to the group." This conclusion is based on a study of older stages of Indoaryan (i.e., Sanskrit) and Iranian (i.e., Avestan, Old Persian) and is difficult to challenge. Thus the lexicostatistical classification in this monograph misses a group that clearly existed.

It is important to realize, however, that the failure to find the Indoiranian group is not due to the lexicostatistical method as such, but is due rather to the self-imposed restriction to *contemporary* word lists (for the reasons described in Section 1.1). Using historical evidence concerning Sanskrit, Avestan, and Old Persian, the lexicostatistical method might well have revealed the Indoiranian group; without such historical evidence, the traditional method might well have failed to find it. In other words, the evidence for this group has been eroded by linguistic change over the millennia, and this erosion is conceivably great enough that contemporary languages fail clearly to reveal the group, whether the data used are lexicostatistical or those of common innovations.

This said, it is of interest to inquire in detail what has obscured the contemporary lexicostatistical evidence for the Indoiranian group. The quality of many of the lists in the Indoiranian area is not above challenge. Furthermore, the range of percentages between Indoaryan and Iranian languages is from 9.4 (Singhalese with Afghan) to 25.4 (Panjabi with Baluchi). Since the range is 16 percentage points, the variability is much higher than is to be expected in a well-defined group and suggests that further study might explain the discrepancy between the performance of the lists and the nonlexicostatistical evidence for an Indoiranian group.

The box diagram in Figure 1 can be interpreted as suggesting widespread problems within both the Indoaryan and Iranian Clusters; the boxes tend to be unduly wide and overlapping. Within Indoaryan some of this effect reflects the behavior of **Nepali List and **Hindi, which tend to have noticeably higher percentages than other lists in their respective groups. This is probably caused by undetected borrowing, so that in Appendix 1 and elsewhere these lists are marked with double asterisks, and their percentages were not used when averaging (see Section 2.3). Outside this the unduly wide boxes within both Indoaryan and Iranian tend to reflect the gross deviation of relatively few percentages. Whereas for example six of the eight percentages appearing in the Indic and East Iranian boxes range over no more than about four percentage points, the two remaining percentages in each box are much lower and increase the ranges by some ten percentage points in each case.

Thus one might wish to consider as more representative the percentages between Indoaryan and Iranian that lie at the higher end of the full range of their percentages. Although these percentages so considered offer some support for an Indoiranian, even the highest of these percentages fail to support an Indoiranian group even as strongly as the Mesoeuropeic Hesion is supported.

Perhaps the explanation for the discrepancy lies in the fact that the entire Indoiranian area, particularly the Iranian area, was increasingly subject to invasion and domination by nonnative groups from the end of the first millennium B.C., the Iranian area by speakers of Arabic among others, and the north Indian area by Iranian speakers led by Mongol rulers. These conquests could have led to intimate borrowing on a sufficiently large scale to have considerably deflated the percentages between Indoaryan and Iranian.

5.2 Slovenian and the Tripartite Division of Slavic

The classification of Slovenian against all other Slavic speech varieties comes as a surprise. It is generally agreed that the Slavic languages are grouped into three varieties, often called Eastern, Western, and Southern, though the membership of these groups is subject to some controversy. The grouping by Van Wijk (1956) does not differ seriously from views that are widely held (for example, see Birnbaum 1966a.194ff.). This grouping divides Slavic into Eastern, Western, and Southern varieties. The eastern varieties are (Van Wijk, 1956.49) Great Russian (here Russian), White Russian (here Byelorussian), and Little Russian (here Ukrainian). The western varieties are (1956.73) Czechoslovak (here Czech, Eastern Czech, and Slovak), Polish, and Sorbian (here Lusatian). Kashubian, not represented here by a list, is by some regarded as a Polish dialect, whereas by others it is considered to be a separate (Pomeranian) dialect. The Southern varieties are (1956.97) Bulgarian, Bulgaro-Serbian (possibly the same as our Macedonian), Serbo-Croatian, and Slovenian.

Van Wijk's classification thus differs markedly in some respects from the classification reached here. Here in the Non-Slovenian group Lusatian, Czechoslovak, Polish, and Russian are coordinate with each other and with our weakly indicated East Central Slavic Hesion consisting of Byelorussian with Ukrainian, as well as with our weakly indicated South Slavic Hesion. The last appears to be the same as Van Wijk's Southern Slavic less Slovenian. It should be noted, however, that the standard classification is predominantly, if not exclusively, based on phonological considerations.

It is plain that the lexicostatistical classification of Slavic given here is sensitive to small changes in the percentages; relatively small changes might have a considerable effect on the classification. This instability would be visible even if there were no traditional classification to compare it with. This internal indication of reliability or unreliability is an advantage of the lexicostatistical method. Obviously, differences between the lexicostatistical and traditional classification are less serious if they occur where the lexicostatistical classification is known by its own internal indicators to be less than usually reliable.

The range of Slovenian percentages with other Slavic lists is narrow compared to the range of percentages within the other Slavic lists, for they range from 61.0 with Byelorussian to 69.4 with Slovak. The last percentage is barely less than the language limit (set at 70%, see Section 1.3), so that the lexicostatistical evidence that Slovenian is a separate Slavic language from Non-Slovenian is weak, and therefore the possibility that Slovenian is, even based on lexicostatistical evidence, a highly aberrant Slavic dialect rather than a separate Slavic language needs to be considered. At the same time, the fact that the percentage Slovenian has with Serbocroatian is no higher than 68.4 points points to a linguistic distance between Slovenian and the Shtokavian variety that is no closer than that between Slovenian and at least some other varieties of Slavic, e.g., Slovak. Certain aspects of this aberrant position of Slovenian are apparently also reflected by Van Wijk who says (1956.110): "We will pass on to the western group, composed of Slovenian and Serbo-Croatian. At present each of these two linguistic territories has its own literary language and these two languages differ so from each other that they are not mutually intelligible without prior acquaintance." However Van Wijk goes on to say (1956.113) that the Kajkavian dialect of Serbo-Croatian, which is not represented in the data of the present work, constitutes a transition toward Slovenian. It is thus not unreasonable to expect that a Kajkavian list would have a higher percentage than the Shtokavian list used here does. If that percentage should be 70 or higher, as is also not unreasonable to expect, the need based on lexicostatistical evidence to consider Slovenian as a separate Slavic language would disappear. In the same sense therefore it is not quite clear whether there is more than one dialectological language among the Slavic speech varieties. In either case, however, Slavic constitutes a distinct group that implies a more homogeneous dialectological language at an earlier period which is called Proto-Slavic.

Within Slavic, the lowest percentage between a pair of lists is 61.0 (between Slovenian and Byelorussian), whereas the highest percentage of a Slavic list with a non-Slavic list is the percentage cited above of 40.4 between Lusatian U and Lithuanian O.

5.3 The Evidence for a Proto-Baltoslavic

The evidence for a Proto-Baltic is as sturdy as that for a Proto-Slavic. Within Baltic the lowest percentage between a pair of lists is 56.1, between Lithuanian O and Latvian, whereas the highest percentage of a Baltic list with a non-Baltic list is 40.4, between Lusatian U and Lithuanian ST.

The hypothesis of a Baltoslavic unity among the Indoeuropean languages is favored by the fact that the highest percentage of any Baltic or Slavic list with a non-Baltoslavic list is 27.1, between Macedonian and Danish, while the smallest percentage between any two Baltoslavic lists is 30.6, between Latvian and Bulgarian. The accidental nature of even this closeness is shown by these facts: (1) Macedonian's highest percentage is 83.5 with Bulgarian, thus setting up the expectation that the percentages of these two lists with less closely related lists should be approximately the same, but Bulgarian scores only 24.0% with Danish, compared with the 27.1% above. (2) Latvian's two highest percentages are with the two Lithuanian lists (61.3, 56.1), leading to a similar expectation, but the Lithuanian lists have percentages 34.2 and 33.5 with Bulgarian, compared with the 30.6 above. Furthermore, these two percentages are typical of the the percentages between Baltic and Slavic lists, since the average of all such percentages is 34.2. (3) The range of percentages of all Baltic lists with all Slavic lists is from 30.6 (Latvian with Bulgarian) to 40.4 (Lithuanian ST with Lusatian U), whereas for example the range of all Baltic lists with all Germanic lists is from 17.5 (Latvian with Faroese) to 23.0 (Lithuanian O with Swedish List) and similarly the range of all Slavic lists with all Germanic lists is from 19.9 (Lusatian U with Faroese) to 27.1 (Macedonian with Danish). The Baltic percentages with Slavic can thus be safely regarded as confirming the hypothesis of a Baltoslavic unity that postdates Proto-Indoeuropean. The language of this unity is called Proto-Baltoslavic.

Since both Baltic and Slavic are subfamilies, their respective percentages with each other as well as with other languages are averaged (as discussed in Section 2.3). It is on this basis that the Baltic Subfamily scores 34.2% with the Slavic Subfamily as reported in Appendix 1.

Many scholars can be cited who support the hypothesis of a Baltoslavic unity; a few of them are A. Vaillant, O. Szemerenyi, and M. Leumann (see Senn 1966.139ff.). Those opposed, and it is safe to say they are in the minority, include A. Senn (1966), A. Salys, whose view is regarded as "well founded" by A. Senn (1966.143), and A. Meillet.

Salys is quoted by Senn (1966) as claiming that the evidence for a Baltoslavic unity can be attributed instead to "their development from two neighboring IE dialects which still remained in contact during the final stages of the disintegration of the Proto-Indo-European unity. The migration of the pre-Balts to the northeast, probably about 2000 B.C., severed the contact with the pre-Slavs and thus led to a separate linguistic development on both sides. A new contact, as late as the 6th century, was established again by the Slavic expansion." In Senn's view, the evidence usually interpreted as implying a Baltoslavic unity is attributed by Salys to a late, dialectalized period of Proto-Indoeuropean, before the latter had ceased to exist as a unitary language, and is thus not evidence for a separate Baltoslavic unity. (Note, incidentally, that the quotation from Salys could perhaps be interpreted differently than Senn does, since "the final stages of disintegration" could be taken to mean that Proto-Indoeuropean had already disintegrated and was no longer a dialectological language, but that some fragments, say including Baltoslavic, were affected by further disintegration.) Senn's interpretation touches on one of the problems that face the attempt to draw inferences from directly determined common innovations. Common innovations can appear as dialectal innovations within a proto-language as well as within one of its well-defined daughter languages. Presumably the decision as to which they are might be made to depend on the magnitude of the common innovations. The larger the number and the weightier the quality of such innovations, the less appealing is the hypothesis that attributes them all to a dialect of the proto-language and the more appealing is the hypothesis that attributes them to the period following the dissolution of the proto-language. In any case serious attention does not appear to have been given to examining carefully the problems faced in attempting to deal with this crux.

Meillet's view (1922.48) is clearly in tune with Salys's position as interpreted by Senn. Meillet concludes "that Baltic and Slavic had exactly identical starting points, that they developed in the same conditions and under the same influences; perhaps they even had a more or less long period of community, but one in which Slavic and Baltic, which are the most conservative Indoeuropean languages, did not introduce any notable innovations ... Baltic and Slavic furnish a fine example of two parallel, but long autonomous developments." Meillet, like Salys as interpreted by Senn, denies any "notable" innovations common to Baltic and Slavic after the dissolution of Proto-Indoeuropean. Although he sees it as conceivable that there might have been a Baltoslavic unity that persisted after the dissolution of Proto-Indoeuropean, he clearly views this possibility as unrelated to the evidence; if a hypothesis is required to explain data, he sees the Baltoslavic hypothesis as otiose.

Senn (1966.143) is ready to "admit the term 'Balto-Slavic' in the sense of 'Baltic and Slavic' and in the meaning of 'Proto-Indo-European of Northeastern Europe in its last phase.' It is the residue of Proto-Indo-European, the remainder left after all adjacent parts had entered into history and developed into independently regulated languages." What Senn leaves unclear is whether he sees his Baltoslavic as a single distinct language (i.e., as a dialectological language). Presumably he wishes to regard Baltic and Slavic as already distinct from each other at the time when they had become distinct from all other Indoeuropean languages, but he is not specific as to whether he finds them distinct *dialects* or distinct *languages*. He disclaims adherence to Meillet's hypothesis of parallel development to explain unifiable innovations that can be found in both Baltic and Slavic (and restricted to them). If Baltic and Slavic were distinct merely as dialects of the same post-Proto-Indoeuropean language, it follows that these common innovations are to be attributed to a Proto-Baltoslavic as it is generally understood; such a Proto-Baltoslavic would, however, make unnecessary his specification of Baltoslavic as meaning merely Baltic and Slavic. If Baltic and Slavic were already distinct as languages at the time in question, then the common innovations could only be assigned to a period in which they together constituted a dialect of Proto-Indoeuropean. Thus Senn's view appears to contain a contradiction. (That Senn's view offers difficulty to others can be seen from the note at the end of his article [1966.150ff.].)

Senn admits, fully or tentatively, six of the fourteen (as counted by Senn) common innovations proposed by Szemerenyi. Once these innovations have been admitted, however, they can bear on the hypothesis of a distinct Baltoslavic unity only if they give evidence that at least some (or even one) appeared after a separate Baltoslavic language had developed. It is thus of some importance to determine how many common innovations could be attributed to a Proto-Baltoslavic. It is such common innovations that are explained by the hypothesis of a

Proto-Baltoslavic; if the hypothesis is to be necessary and sufficient, not all of the proposed agreements restricted to Baltic and Slavic can be innovations reasonably attributable to a dialect of a dialectalized Proto-Indoeuropean rather than to a daughter language. It is of course possible to take the position that such a determination is possible only in rare instances. Nevertheless it seems reasonable to work with the principle that the larger the number of determinable shared innovations, the greater the likelihood that at least one is associated with a distinct language. But in the absence of a method of evaluating the weight of the number of the proposed agreements as evidence for or against one of the two possibilities, it would appear to be of some importance that the lexicostatistical evidence preeminently favors the hypothesis of a separate Baltoslavic unity.

5.4 Mesoeuropeic, Italoceltic, and Northwestern Indoeuropean

An argument like that favoring proto-Baltoslavic can be developed in reverse in relation to the hypothesis of an Italoceltic unity. Meillet (1922.33) concludes that "before the Italic unity, there was a still more distant and less easily determinable unity, the Italo-Celtic unity." C. Watkins (1966.49) on the other hand says, after discussing Meillet's arguments, "... but in no sense have we spoken, or should we speak, of an Italo-Celtic unity, either as a language, or as a culture." W. Cowgill (1970.143) essentially agrees with this position, saying in regard to the exclusive shared innovations of Italic and Celtic, "... the four[5] that I have discussed in this paper ... while hardly enough to establish a real subgroup, do seem to require a time when Italic and Celtic were closer to each other than either was to any neighboring dialect of which significant material has survived. But this period of contact seems to have been broken off very early ... ."

Cowgill thus attributes the determinable common Italic and Celtic innovations to a period when the respective antecedents of Proto-Italic and Proto-Celtic were in a dialectal relationship with each other and the antecedents of other languages, in particular that of Proto-Germanic. Although he depicts the antecedent of Proto-Germanic as exhibiting

---

5. Cowgill appears to have omitted from the count the point he himself makes (1970.142) that "Italic and Celtic innovated together in creating a 1st pl. medio-passive **-mor...*," which would be a fifth exclusively shared innovation.

contacts of its own with other dialects to the east and south, it is not quite clear whether the last period at which this was true is to be dated as in Proto-Indoeuropean or after its dissolution. In any case the same problem appears of distinguishing between common innovations which are to be attributed to a dialect of a proto-language and those to be attributed to a daughter language of that proto-language. Only the latter are valid for an argument in support of a well-defined group; at the same time it must be kept in mind that the nonappearance of a feature in the successors of other dialects of the proto-language could be due to loss in one or more daughter languages. Even if it be conceded in agreement with Cowgill that the common innovations that he finds are not so many and/or so weighty as to require the hypothesis of an Italoceltic unity, it must be conceded that the Italoceltic hypothesis has not been actually contraindicated by these considerations.

For this reason it could be regarded as of some importance that the lexicostatistical evidence contraindicates an Italoceltic unity. In fact the lexicostatistical evidence seems to favor the hypothesis that Celtic separated from Italic (the antecedent of Latin and the Romance languages) much before Italic separated from Germanic and Baltoslavic. Since the lexicostatistical evidence favors, however weakly, an Italic-Germanic-Baltoslavic unity that not unlikely persisted after the dissolution of Proto-Indoeuropean, this group is included in the classification and called Mesoeuropeic.

A group containing precisely Italic, Germanic, and Baltoslavic is not one that has wide support, if indeed it has ever been proposed before. However, Meillet (1922.23) has suggested that there was evidence in the vocabulary restricted to the northwestern Indoeuropean languages (Slavic, Baltic, Germanic, Celtic, and Italic) which appears to result "from a common cultural development," presumably apart from the other Indoeuropean languages. He reaches this conclusion on the basis of approximately 55 cognate sets. Of these, however, only about 35 include a Celtic cognate so that there would appear to be as much evidence for considering a "common cultural development" for a central European (Mesoeuropeic) set of languages as for a northwestern set. Although Meillet restricts his hypothesis to a "common culture," the evidence is not restricted to words with "cultural" meanings; rather it includes some with "basic" meanings. Consequently it seems reasonable to consider his hypothesis as tantamount to proposing an Indoeuropean group even though he does not actually do so.

It is now worthwhile examining the lexicostatistical evidence that excludes Celtic from Mesoeuropeic. There are reasons for believing that the percentages of Celtic with outside languages are deflated. Welsh and Breton have a relatively large number of borrowings in their respective vocabularies from Latin and the Romance languages. If such borrowings appear in our word lists (which is likely for intimate borrowing), they tend to deflate percentages (see Section 2.4 and Dyen 1963.64). Furthermore the Irish A list tends to have lower percentages than the Irish B list (for reasons which are not clear), so that there is some reason to suspect that the Irish B list is a better representative for the present purposes than the Irish A list. Additionally both Irish lists seem to have consistently lower percentages with non-Celtic languages than the Welsh and Breton lists. If the true critical percentage of Celtic were about two percentage points higher (and continued to be shared with Romance), there might then have been good reason for considering Celtic a member of the Mesoeuropeic Hesion and for thus reaching the group of northwestern languages suggested by Meillet.

5.5 English

It is not unlikely that the percentages of English with other Germanic languages are similarly deflated by intimate borrowing from French, and accordingly the weakly supported Continental Germanic Hesion without English is quite likely spurious, yet the historical events leading to an acceptance of the traditional classification are themselves not clear-cut. The English percentages clearly fail to agree with the widely accepted classification of English as a member with Dutch-German in a "West Germanic" subgroup that excludes Nordic. It should perhaps be noted that the support for the generally accepted classification of English directly with Dutch-German can not include common innovations that predate the linguistic split between West Germanic and Nordic, since these can have no bearing on the priority of this split over that between English and Dutch-German. Although it is well known that the source of English is from Dutch-German (i.e., West Germanic) territory, it does not necessarily follow that the separation of English as a dialectological language postdated the separation of Nordic from Dutch-German. The lexicostatistical evidence on its face favors the view that the separation of English predated that of Nordic. However, the separation of English from Dutch-German due to mutual unintelligibility might reasonably be dated about two centuries after the Norman conquest, whereas the Nordic separation concerns events at the base of the Jutland Peninsula in Schleswig-Holstein.

There appears to be general agreement that there is a "sharply defined difference between West Germanic and Scandinavian, which border each other in the Jutland Peninsula" (Bloomfield 1933.314; see also 1933.53). Presumably this difference arose as the result of the meeting of mutually unintelligible Germanic dialects advancing from the north and/or from the south over territory occupied either originally or concurrently by transitional dialects. The geographical linguistic boundary was the consequence of their meeting; the former connection by a chain of pairs of mutually intelligible dialects no longer existed because the speakers had decamped or were absorbed. The dialects that met had earlier on become, one is compelled to believe, mutually unintelligible, for if they had been mutually intelligible, a transitional dialect would almost certainly have developed between them. But just when the elimination of the transition between Nordic and Dutch-German occurred is difficult to determine from the literature. One senses that setting this event before A.D. 1000 would probably meet with the approval of some scholars, whereas others might wish to set it much later. Only if the date were set before English became mutually unintelligible with all the rest of West Germanic would the lexicostatistical result be in error. Even though it may be considered an error, it seems clear that the error must be regarded as small one if for no other reason than that it is difficult to demonstrate.

5.6 English and Frisian (The Ingveonic Hypothesis)

A number of scholars regard English as most closely related to Frisian (see Meillet and Cohen 1952.60, Bloomfield 1933.58) among the West Germanic speech varieties and to form with it an Ingveonic group. The evidence for this view is partly historical, for it is believed that Frisians were among the invaders of England, say as the Jutes and the Anglians (see Jespersen 1972.32ff.), and thus contributed to the formation of English. The other evidence is the claim that Frisian or some Frisian dialects show marked resemblances to English, as in Jespersen's suggestion (1972.18) that "Frisian and English seem more naturally to be considered a separate group intermediate between the first three (i.e., High German, Dutch, Low German [= Plattdeutsch]) and the Scandinavian languages." However, Meillet and Cohen (1952.59-60) treat West Germanic as having German and English as its principal representatives and German as comprising High German and Low German; Low German for its part is composed of Plattdeutsch, Dutch, and Frisian. In such a classification the generally accepted view that Plattdeutsch and Dutch are connected by transitional dialects could be taken to imply that Frisian was similarly connected to them by transitional dialects and was thus part of Meillet and Cohen's German, i.e., our Dutch-German. To further complicate the problem from the lexicostatistical side, the fact that the Frisian list used is from the Netherlands could be taken to suggest that its high percentage with Dutch could be due at least in part to undetected borrowings.

Indeed the fact that Frisian shares 82.2% with Dutch as its critical percentage would agree with Meillet and Cohen's classification. With such a high percentage the chances of mutual intelligibility are quite high; nevertheless instances of even higher percentages associated with mutual unintelligibility have been found (see Section 1.3) and it is therefore not impossible that Frisian is a separate West Germanic language (see Bloomfield 1933.58). Since Frisian seems to be generally regarded as a different language from Dutch and there is no explicit statement to the contrary, Frisian is treated here as an independent language. Only under this condition would it be possible to consider Jespersen's suggestion above to put English together with Frisian against Nordic and Dutch-German.

If indeed Frisian is distinct from Dutch-German, the date of the actual linguistic separation (not the mere physical separation) of English from Frisian needs to be later than that of Frisian from Dutch-German in order to justify classifying English with Frisian and thus forming the Ingveonic group. If Frisian's separation from Dutch-German is taken to have occurred after the separation of English from Frisian, the Ingveonic hypothesis is contradicted. The Ingveonic hypothesis requires that English and Frisian should have continued to be mutually intelligible after Frisian ceased to be connected with any Dutch-German dialect by mutual intelligibility or transitional dialects. If that requirement is not met, the only support for the Ingveonic hypothesis is the premise that English originated by a migratory separation from the area of the chain constituting its common ancestor with Frisian, at that time a dialect of their common ancestor with Dutch-German. Since this separation by general agreement concerns co-dialects rather than different dialectological languages, it is here regarded as insufficient to establish the Ingveonic hypothesis. From a classificatory point of view, the closest relative of a language is the *language* most recently mutually intelligible with it.

In connection with the historical claim of the association of English with West Germanic one should also consider Jespersen's view (1972.60) that "an Englishman would have no difficulty in understanding a Viking — nay, we have positive evidence that Norse people looked upon the English language as one with their own." He seems to take the fact that "Wulfistan speaks of the invaders as 'people who do not know your language'" as merely an indication that the two speech varieties were noticeably dissimilar, not mutually unintelligible. Since the Vikings were fresh from Denmark, this mutual intelligibility would inevitably have extended to their homeland's speech and might then have persisted through Knut's reign and even into the period immediately following the Norman conquest. It is thus conceivable that Anglo-Saxon was a link connecting continental West Germanic with Nordic after all other links of mutual intelligibility had disappeared. Such a history is not being asserted here (though it is not far from Jespersen's view in 1972.18), but it is apparently neither impossible nor easy to refute by evidence. It is not our purpose to insist on such a history, but rather to indicate that the lexicostatistical percentages raise some interesting points and at the very least can be regarded as reasonably approximative of whatever was the true course of events, even if not perfectly accurate.

In fact the failure of the lexicostatistical method to separate Scandinavian from Dutch-German before the latter separated from English may very well be due at least in part to undetected borrowing, and if so, probably from Plattdeutsch into Danish. Jespersen (1972.60) indicates a "powerful foreign influence" on "Danish from Low German."

5.7 Gujarati

Although the lexicostatistical classification unites Gujarati and Marathi in a Marathic Cluster, Voegelin and Voegelin (1977.164) speak of a "genuine boundary between Marathi, on the one hand, and Gujarati, Rajasthani, Western Hindi, and Eastern Hindi on the other." Furthermore they seem to suggest that the latter group are interconnected by transitional dialects. The lexicostatistical percentage 61.3 that connects Marathi and Gujarati is compatible with their sharing a language boundary. However, the percentage 55.2 connecting Gujarati with the Hindic Subfamily (the group here that approximates the Voegelin and Voegelin group above associated with Gujarati) would fit more easily with the appearance of another language boundary separating Gujarati from the others. On the other hand it is not impossible that there is a long chain of transitional dialects making the indicated connection.

6. THE BOX DIAGRAM AND DISCREPANCIES

In every field of science it is useful and important to search for discrepancies between the available data and what is known or believed. For example, after Grimm's Law had been established, an examination of the exceptions to this law led to the discovery of Verner's Law. Examples in other sciences are common. Though we cannot expect to achieve results as memorable as with Verner's Law, it is in the same spirit that we systematically search for discrepancies. It is an advantage of the lexicostatistical method that it permits a more systematic approach to finding several kinds of discrepancies than does the traditional method.

Discrepancies between the lexicostatistical and traditional classifications were covered in Chapter 5. In the present section, the focus is on discrepancies between the lexicostatistical classification and the lexicostatistical percentages on which it is based. Since there is good reason to believe that the lexicostatistical classification is the one most appropriate for the lexicostatistical percentages, these discrepancies should arise only to the extent that the percentages do not conform to the constraints of the family tree model, as discussed in Section 2.1.

The present search for discrepancies in Figure 1 is based on the two properties in the family tree model (see Section 2.1). According to the first property, as explained below, for each box in Figure 1 the lexicostatistical percentages that "belong" to that box should be equal, *except* for the effects of random variation on the percentages. This means that width of each box should be zero except for the extent to which random variation widens the box. This requires the examination of the widths of the boxes to see if they are acceptable. According to the second property, as explained below, if group A is a subgroup of group B then the percentages within group A should be larger than the percentages within group B, except insofar as the effect of random variation may cause some some exceptions. This means that the box for group A should be to the entirely to the left of the box for group B in Figure 1, and hence the boxes should not overlap, except due to random variation. This requires examination of the overlaps of boxes to see if they are acceptable.

First consider the widths of the boxes. Although it is practical on the basis of statistical theory to calculate what the random variation of the lexicostatistical percentages should be, it is unfortunately difficult (using either theoretical calculation or simulation) to go on and calculate using the family tree model what the random variation of the box widths should be. For this reason, an informal nonstatistical approach is used to to examine the box widths, starting in the second paragraph below. The remainder of this paragraph presents the theoretical random variation of the percentages, using theory and results from Kruskal, Dyen, and Black (1973), since these values provide some informal guidance concerning the size of the random variation of the box widths. The following paragraph gives a brief account of how these values are obtained. if P_{ij} is the lexicostatistical percentage connecting languages i and j, then the theoretical standard deviation sij of P_{ij} lies between 2.2 and 3.1 percentage points in virtually all circumstances. (Unfortunately, the several percentages that belong to a box and define its width are not independent, which is part of the reason it is difficult to calculate the random variation of box width.) Also note that many percentages discussed in this monograph connect two *groups* rather than two speech varieties and result from averaging many values (see Section 2.3). Such percentages may be subject to far smaller random variation, though it would be difficult to find out how small by theoretical calculation or by simulation.

(For readers interested in the method used to derive the preceding figures, here is a brief account. The lexicostatistical percentage P_{ij} can be thought of as the average of 200 variables L_{mij}, where $m = 1$ to 200 indicates the Swadesh meaning and where L_{mij} is 1 if the words for meaning M in languages i and j are cognate and is 0 otherwise. If the replacement rate over time for meaning m is r_m and the time separation between languages i and j is t_{ij}, then L_{mij} has probability $\exp(-r_m t_{ij})$ of being 1. From the replacement rates r_m for Indoeuropean in the paper cited, straightforward calculation yields sij as a function of t_{ij}. As t_{ij} goes from 0 to infinity, this function rises from 0 to a maximum of 3.1 percentage points, and then decreases toward 0. The maximum occurs near 0.5 time units $\approx$ 1700 years. For t_{ij} very small, namely 0.2 time units $\approx$ 340 years, and for t_{ij} very large, namely, 2 time units $\approx$ 6,800 years, sij is 2.2 percentage points.)

Now we start a simple common-sense approach to examining box widths. Table 3a shows box widths for 34 groups, and lists them in alphabetical order. Before starting to examine these widths, however, several paragraphs are used to explain the exact meaning of numerical width as shown in the table, and to explain in detail the statements above about how the two assumptions of the family tree model relate to the

Table 3a

BOX WIDTHS BY NAME

"—" means no entry. "=" means equal entry

Name of Group	Width with deviant percentages excluded (dicussion)	included (Fig. 1)
Albanian	.032	=
Baltic Subfamily	.052	=
Baltoslavic Subfamily	.098	=
Breton	.061	=
Brythonic Subfamily	.031	=
Celtic Subfamily	.051	=
Continental Germanic Hesion	.164	=
Czechoslovakian Cluster	.009	=
Demotic Greek	.055	=
Dutch	.016	=
Dutch-German	.138	=
East Iranian Hesion	.145	=
Franco-Provençal Cluster	.060	=
Gangetic Hesion	.092	.177
Germanic Subfamily	.072	.155
Greek	—	.077
Hindic	—	.031
Iberian	.012	=
Indic Subfamily	.063	.131
Indoaryan Cluster	.104	.151
Indoeuropean Family	.173	.186
Iranian Cluster	.107	=
Mesoeuropeic Hesion	.096	.128
Non-Slovenian Slavic	.199	=
Nordic	.042	=
Nuclear Albanian	.040	=
Persic Subfamily	.110	=
Romance Subfamily	.149	.188
South Slavic Hesion	.126	=
Scandinavian Cluster	.065	=
Sindhic Subfamily	.080	.211
Slavic Subfamily	.084	=
Swedish Hesion	.021	=
Western Romance Subfamily	.206	.284

Table 3b

BOX WIDTHS BY RANK

All boxes that "have width".

Deviant percentages excluded. See text re overlap

Name of Group	Width	Rank order	Overlap?
Western Romance Subfamily	.206	32	yes
Non-Slovenian Slavic	.199	31	yes
Indoeuropean Family	.173	30	yes
Continental Germanic Hesion	.164	29	yes
Romance Subfamily	.149	28	yes
East Iranian Hesion	.145	27	yes
Dutch-German	.138	26	
South Slavic Hesion	.126	25	yes
Persic Subfamily	.110	24	yes
Iranian Cluster	.107	23	yes
Indoaryan Cluster	.104	22	yes
Baltoslavic Subfamily	.098	21	
Mesoeuropeic Hesion	.096	20	yes
Gangetic Hesion	.092	19	yes
Slavic Subfamily	.084	18	yes
Sindhic Subfamily	.080	17	yes
Germanic Subfamily	.072	16	yes
Scandinavian Cluster	.065	15	yes
Indic Subfamily	.063	14	
Breton	.061	13	
Franco-Provençal Cluster	.060	12	
Demotic Greek	.055	11	
Baltic Subfamily	.052	10	
Celtic Subfamily	.051	9	
Nordic	.042	8	yes
Nuclear Albanian	.040	7	
Albanian	.032	6	
Brythonic Subfamily	.031	5	
Swedish Hesion	.021	4	
Dutch	.016	3	
Iberian	.012	2	
Czechoslovakian Cluster	.009	1	

boxes in Figure 1.

The *width* of a box shown in Table 3a is the difference between the maximum and minimum percentages that belong to the box. For example, the three percentages that belong to Breton are 88.8, 92.9, and 94.9: therefore the width of the Breton box is $6.1 = 94.9 - 88.8$. The visual width is slightly larger, due to the space between the lines of the box and the symbols it contains, and due to the thickness of the lines themselves.

In Table 3a, the two columns for widths reflect the existence of deviant groups, lists, and percentages. In Section 2.4 certain percentages associated with certain lists and groups were identified as deviant and given special treatment during the subgrouping procedure. The groups and lists involved are these:

> **Albanian [Subfamily], **French Creole [Subfamily],
> **French Creole C, **French Creole D,
> **Greek K (**Katharevousa), **Hindi, **Nepali List,
> **Takitaki.

Unfortunately, Figure 1 was made without allowance for the special treatment of the deviant percentages, lists, and groups, and it was not practical subsequently to make a new version correcting this oversight. To help the reader deal with the differences between Figure 1 and the following discussion, Table 3a was constructed to show the widths, with one column excluding and another column including the deviant percentages.

A group which contains only two speech varieties has only one percentage. Thus its width is necessarily 0, and there is nothing to be examined in the present context. A group like this is said to *have no width*, while any other group *has width*. Table 3a shows all 34 groups that have width when deviant percentages are included, and lists them in alphabetical order. Of these groups, nine show widths that differ according to whether deviant percentages are excluded or included. In several groups, such as Germanic and Sindhic, the widths differ a great deal. Most other groups have identical values whether or not the deviant percentages are included, because no deviant percentages are present in the associated box. Of the 34 groups, two have no width when deviant percentages are excluded, namely, Greek and Hindic. After excluding the deviant percentages which link **Katharevousa (**Greek K) to the other Greek dialects, there are no percentages at all left in the Greek box, and after excluding the deviant percentages involving **Hindi, there is only one percentage left in the Hindic box.

Table 3b shows the 32 groups that have width when deviant percentages are excluded, and lists them in descending order of width. The column labeled "Rank order" shows the rank order value of the width. When it is useful in the following discussion, the name of a group is accompanied by the number denoting the rank order value of its width as a clear indication of its position in Table 3b. The column labeled "Overlap?" indicates whether or not the associated box overlaps another box.

As indicated above, the search for discrepancies using Figure 1 is based on the two properties in the family tree model. According to the first property, as described in Section 2.1, the lexicostatistical percentages for all pairs of coordinate speech varieties within a group should be equal, except for random variation. For example, the pairs of coordinate dialects in the Celtic group all involve one Irish dialect and one Brythonic dialect, and have the following percentages:

	Breton List	Breton SE	Breton ST	Welsh N	Welsh C
Irish A	31.1	30.9	31.9	34.4	34.2
Irish B	33.5	32.1	32.8	35.5	36.0

The minimum and maximum values in this table are 30.9 and 36.0. The statistical *range* of these ten values is the difference, 5.1, between minimum and maximum, which is called here the *width* of the Celtic box. These ten values were taken from the big table in Appendix 5, but can also be read off approximately from the entries in the Celtic box of Figure 1. According to the family tree model, all these values should be equal except for random variation. The same is true for other boxes. Thus according to the family tree model, the width of each box should be due entirely to random variation of the percentages.

The second property in the family tree model states that if group A is a subgroup of group B, then the percentages within group A should be larger than the percentages within group B. For example, Breton is a subgroup of Brythonic. The range of percentages within each group are as follows:

Breton: from 88.8 to 94.9.
Brythonic: from 61.0 to 64.1.

According to the family tree model, the former numbers are all expected to be larger than the latter numbers, as indeed they are. In terms of Figure 1, this means that the Breton box should be to the left of the Brythonic box as it is, since the percentage scale in the figure has larger values to the left. Thus two boxes should never overlap, except to a limited degree due to random variation in the percentages. Also, one box should never contain another, except possibly close to the edge, since inclusion is a form of overlapping. (To be precise, two boxes are said to overlap if one or more percentages that belong to one of the boxes are also within the other box. The technical argument that justifies the statement about overlapping is that if two boxes overlap, then they share channels, so the groups corresponding to the boxes share speech varieties. In a hierarchical classification, two groups cannot share speech varieties unless one is a subgroup of the other.) Thus any sufficiently large overlap is a possible discrepancy calling for investigation. While a rigorous specification of "sufficiently large" is difficult to work out, a standard deviation of 2 or 3 percentage points is shown above for each separate percentage, so it is clear that a box overlap of 2 or 3 percentage points is certainly not too large.

Now we resume the examination of discrepancies from the family tree model. We start by using the second property, according to which any sufficiently large overlap is a discrepancy. Figure 1 shows all 18 overlaps, but only 13 are left when five overlaps disappear after exclusion of the deviant percentages,[6] as shown in Table 4.

This table names the overlapping boxes in the left-hand and right-hand columns. The 13 overlaps involve 18 distinct groups, 17 of which have width and are marked "yes" in the "Overlap?" column of Table 3b. Western Sardinian Hesion in the bottom line of Table 4 does not have

6. Here are the five overlaps that disappear after exclusion of the deviant percentages: Indic Subfamily with Sindhic Subfamily; Indic Subfamily with Gangetic Hesion; Sindhic Subfamily with Marathic Cluster; Gangetic Hesion with Marathic Cluster; and Western Romance Subfamily with Franco-Provençal Cluster. Among the 13 overlaps that remain, removal of the deviant percentages causes the amount of overlap to be reduced in four cases.

Table 4

Group name	Rank order	Over-lap	Rank order	Group name
Non-Slovenian Slavic	31	12.1	25	South Slavic Hesion
Indoeuropean Family	30	8.4	23	Iranian Cluster
Indoeuropean Family	30	7.9	20	Mesoeuropeic Hesion
Indoeuropean Family	30	6.8	22	Indoaryan Cluster
Iranian Cluster	23	6.7	27	East Iranian Hesion
Germanic Subfamily	16	6.5	29	Continental Germanic H.
Slavic Subfamily	18	6.3	31	Non-Slovenian Slavic
Indoeuropean Family	30	4.4	27	East Iranian Hesion
Sindhic Subfamily	17	4.2	19	Gangetic Hesion
Romance Subfamily	28	3.4	32	Western Romance Subf.
Nordic	8	1.2	15	Scandinavian Cluster
East Iranian Hesion	27	.3	24	Persic Subfamily
Western Romance S.	32	.0	—	Western Sardinian H.

width. Table 4 shows the amount of overlap in the central column. For each group, the table shows next to the name its rank in the order of widths, taken from Table 3b. The table is arranged in order of decreasing amount of overlap.

Now the "Overlap?" column of Table 4 shows that there is a strong association between overlapping and wide boxes. For one thing, the 18 distinct boxes that show overlap consist of the 18 widest boxes from rank 32 down to rank 15, except that two of these boxes, Dutch-German (rank 26) and Baltoslavic (rank 21), are missing, while two other boxes are present, Nordic (rank 8) and Western Sardinian, a box without width. For another, the 8 largest overlaps between boxes each involve at least one of the 6 widest groups (i.e., each overlap ≥ 4.4 involves at least one group with rank ≥ 27). Also, when the overlaps are examined one by one, in almost every case of more than a slight overlap one or both boxes involved is quite wide. For example, within Romance both overlaps involve the widest box, Western Romance box (WR). Within Germanic, the overlap between the Germanic box and the Continental Germanic box (CG) involves the fourth widest box, while the overlap between Scandinavian (Scv) and Nordic, which are not wide, is slight. Within Baltoslavic, both overlaps involve the Non-Slovenian box (NS), which is the second widest box. Indoaryan and Iranian provide further examples.

Thus even though it is difficult to assess directly whether the widest boxes are too wide or not, the wider boxes are associated with overlaps, most of which probably indicate discrepancies from the family tree model. Hence the wider boxes in themselves presumably indicate discrepancies. The next step is to attempt to find the possible causes of these discrepancies.

One conceivable cause is that the classification in this monograph is not the one which best fits the lexicostatistical percentages. In the present situation this possibility is considered to be remote for several reasons. First, the classification was constructed by a reasonable, systematic method, as described in Section 2.2. Second, during the construction of the classification, the percentages and the joining steps were examined with care for anomalies and peculiarities which might be caused by known linguistic phenomena. Several such anomalies were found and dealt with, as described in Section 2.4. Third, plausible alternative classifications were constructed and the associated box diagrams plotted for various parts of the tree where the discrepancies occur, and it was found that they did not reduce the discrepancies. Fourth, classifications were calculated by alternative subgrouping procedures, and the results compared with the classification in this monograph, as described in Section 2.1.

Therefore it may safely be concluded that it is not possible for any family tree (see Section 2.1) describing these percentages to avoid limited discrepancies from the family tree model. In other words, the family tree model is not capable of giving a perfect description of these lexicostatistical percentages. This should not be surprising, for it has been clear to linguists for many years that the family tree model is overly simplistic. Dialectal variation and diffusion can affect languages in ways that must cause discrepancies between any classification (whether or not it is based on lexicostatistical percentages) and the family tree model. However, limited discrepancies do not mean that the family tree model needs to be abandoned. Rather it is still an excellent first approximation, and the discrepancies mean only that the model needs to be refined.

It is hard to avoid the conclusion that the discrepancies discussed in this section are due to the fact that descendants from certain proto-languages in the family tree developed *not* in accordance with the family tree model but rather by dialectal variation and diffusion. (While unnoticed errors such as undetected borrowing may perhaps exist in the cognations, they could only be responsible for a small part of the observed discrepancies.) A technique known as multidimensional scaling is now available to represent the relationship between speech varieties with parsimony and simplicity approaching that of a family tree, though the form of the representation is completely different from a family tree. Applications of this technique, which can easily be used with lexicostatistical percentages, are given in Chapter 7.

7. MULTIDIMENSIONAL SCALING

As described in Section 2.1, the method used to find the lexicostatistical classification of Indoeuropean is based on the goal of describing the lexicostatistical percentages by a family tree model. The use of open groups, a somewhat ad hoc device that handles some deviation from this model, does not change this basic fact. Although the family tree model has had great success in historical linguistics, it is well known that there are a few groups, such as Slavic, Romance, and Indoeuropean, for which the branches immediately below the group cannot be satisfactorily described with this model. Though hierarchical classification of such groups based on the family tree model turns out to have considerable value and to be more useful than no classification at all, that does not remove its flaws.

The reason why the family tree model can satisfactorily describe the branches immediately below some groups, such as Celtic, and not below other groups, such as Slavic, has to do with the accidents of history. Consider a group G and the groups (or dialects) A, B, C, etc. immediately beneath it, and call the corresponding speech varieties Proto-G and Proto-A, Proto-B, etc. Consider the several development processes that lead from Proto-G to each of Proto-A, Proto-B, etc. (Note that Proto-G may also have other descendent speech varieties. If so, they do not correspond to known groups or dialects, perhaps because they subsequently died out or were not documented.) If the development processes take place in geographical isolation from each other for the great majority of their lifetimes, then the relationship between the subtrees headed by A, B, etc. can usually be given a satisfactory description by the family tree model. On the other hand, if large parts of the development lifetimes take place within a single intercommunicating region R (possibly containing other dialects of G as well), so that geographical waves of change may affect some but not all the speech varieties involved, then the family tree model usually does not give a satisfactory description of this part of the tree.

Consider a portion of the Indoeuropean tree where the family tree (however obtained) is observed to be less than fully adequate, such as the branches immediately beneath the Slavic group, or the Romance group, or the Indoeuropean group. A better approach to classification in such instances requires a nonhierarchical approach of some kind. The fact that the inadequacy apparently stems from wave or diffusion effects, which

FIGURE 2. **Pseudomap of Slavic Languages.**

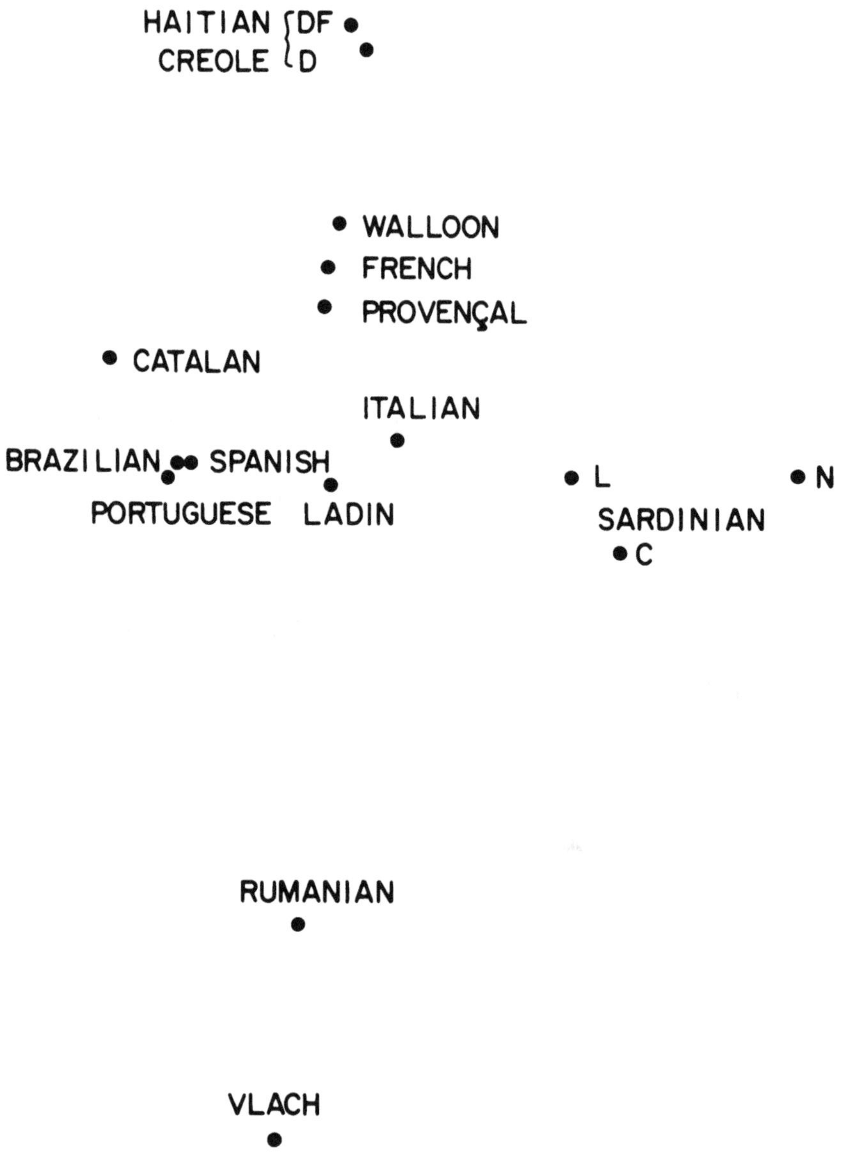

HAITIAN {DF
CREOLE {D

WALLOON
FRENCH
PROVENÇAL
CATALAN
ITALIAN
BRAZILIAN SPANISH
PORTUGUESE LADIN
L
N
SARDINIAN
C

RUMANIAN

VLACH

FIGURE 3. **Pseudomap of Romance Languages.**

are geographical, suggests using some sort of spatially oriented classification to supplement the hierarchical classification.

Black (1976) has approached classification based on lexicostatistical percentages through the method of "multidimensional scaling," which is often abbreviated as MDS. Instead of a hierarchical classification, this method produces map-like representations of the linguistic relationships, such as those shown in Figures 2 and 3. These figures are referred to here as "pseudomaps," though they are usually referred to as configurations in the MDS literature.

Each speech variety is represented on a pseudomap by a point. As we saw at the beginning of Chapter 2, the lexicostatistical method is based on the simple principle that the lexicostatistical percentage indicates the degree of relatedness between two speech varieties. The same principle is used here. Informally, the idea is to use physical distance in the pseudomap to inversely represent degree of relatedness, which is given by the lexicostatistical percentage. Speech varieties such as Byelorussian and Russian that have a high percentage and are relatively similar to each other should be close together on the pseudomap, whereas speech varieties such as Byelorussian and Bulgarian that have a lower percentage and are relatively dissimilar should be relatively far apart on the pseudomap. Multidimensional scaling is simply a systematic computational method of creating such a pseudomap by placing points on a piece of paper (i.e., a 2-dimensional space) in such a way that they reflect the relative degrees of similarity as well as possible. (Note that "similar" and "dissimilar" are understood only as *relative* terms: among the Slavic dialects displayed on Figure 2, Byelorussian and Bulgarian are *relatively* dissimilar, and have a *relatively* low percentage, despite the close relationship they enjoy in an absolute sense.) More formally, multidimensional scaling is based on a spatial model which is not spelled out here, but can be found in the references cited below.

Pseudomaps need not be in two-dimensional space but can be in n-dimensional space for n = 1, 2, 3, or more, as the word "multidimensional" indicates. In practice, however, the dimensionality n is seldom larger than 3, and is most often 2. The dimensionality is chosen by the user of MDS, almost always after trying several different values, but is strongly influenced by the data. The results from applying MDS to a data set with several values of n frequently yield indications interpretable by an expert data analyst as to whether one of the values tried for n is an appropriate value. For the data sets presented in this chapter, two dimensions ($n = 2$) turn out to be appropriate in every case, with the partial exception of the data for the major branches of Indoeuropean, where it is difficult to decide whether $n = 2$ or 3 is more appropriate.

In summary, multidimensional scaling is a statistical method which makes use of numerical measures of similarity such as lexicostatistical percentages in order to produce a pseudomap. Descriptions of MDS are available in numerous places. Black (1976) gives an elementary account intended for linguists, as well as linguistic applications, but his article is not so easily available. A short and *very* elementary account can be found in Kruskal (1972 and 1978). Kruskal and Wish (1978) is an elementary account widely used by social scientists. Carroll and Kruskal (1978) is somewhat more advanced and fairly easily available. In practice, MDS is always carried out with the aid of a computer program, and there are several programs which are widely used for this purpose. The applications described here used two very similar programs called MDSCAL and KYST, which are available from AT&T Bell Laboratories at Murray Hill, New Jersey, and whose numerical methods are fully documented in Kruskal (1977).

The multidimensional scaling model is not intended to compete with the family tree model. Instead, the pseudomap produced by the former is intended to *supplement* the family tree produced by the latter. It does so by covering certain situations where the family tree does not and cannot provide an adequate description of the actual linguistic relationships, because there is gradual dialectal variation resulting from the fact that dialect features may spread from one dialect to another by contact. Furthermore, unlike a family tree, a single pseudomap does not and cannot describe the languages at many different points in time. One pseudomap can only describe the relationship between the immediate descendants of one group in the family tree.

When seeking to interpret a pseudomap, it is important to understand that the pseudomap has neither absolute scale nor absolute orientation. It does not have an absolute scale because it uses only relative sizes of the input similarities; and it does not have an absolute orientation because distance on a pseudomap doesn't change if the map is rotated or turned over. Thus one is free to rotate, enlarge, diminish, and/or turn over a pseudomap when seeking to interpret what it means. This freedom has been used in the following comparisons, to make each pseudomap resemble as nearly as possible the corresponding real map.

It is also important not to expect perfect agreement between a pseudomap and a real map, since there are many valid reasons for discrepancies between them. Thus in the following comparisons, the approximate resemblances between pseudomaps and real maps clearly demonstrate that the number of lexical innovations separating two dialects is approximately proportional to the geographic distance between the two dialects, which is of course consistent with spreading by diffusion based on contact. The tiny number of dialects that appear in the "wrong" places on the pseudomaps presumably reflect special factors that have speeded up or slowed down such diffusion in special cases. One such factor is the loss of mutual intelligibility with the adjacent dialects, which was presumably the case with Slovenian as discussed below. Another special factor was identified in an example in Black (1976), where the pseudomap placed coastal dialects closer together and inland dialects further apart, relative to each other, than the real map. Black identifies the special factor as good water transport versus difficult overland transport due to rugged terrain. Discrepancies between the pseudomap and the real map should be seen not as errors but as phenomena for which an explanation is sought, though of course we cannot hope to explain every such discrepancy any more than linguists can explain every discrepancy from the standard sound correspondences (such as the form of the English word "egg").

Figure 2 is a pseudomap for the Slavic Subfamily, obtained by applying the KYST program to the lexicostatistical percentages connecting these dialects. Figure 3 is the corresponding pseudomap for the Romance Subfamily. Each point represents one dialect, as shown. The relative distance between each pair of points reflects the relative lexical dissimilarity or similarity between the corresponding dialects. More specifically, there is a strong inverse relationship between *lexicostatistical percentage* and *distance*. If the percentage is large the distance is small; and if the percentage is small the distance is large.

The next two paragraphs give a very brief description of one method for calculating the multidimensional pseudomap or configuration. The KYST and MDSCAL programs construct the pseudomap using a quantity called "stress." Stress is calculated from the percentages and the distances, and measures how far the pseudomap deviates from having a perfect inverse relationship. An ideal pseudomap would have zero stress, and the larger the stress the worse the pseudomap is. However, for most sets of data it is not possible to obtain a pseudomap with zero stress; just how small it is possible to make the stress depends on the data and the dimensionality of the pseudomap (and on other factors too technical to discuss here). If the smallest stress obtainable for a given data set in a given dimensionality *n* is large, then the pseudomap in *n* dimensions does not reflect the data well, and the pseudomap is unlikely to be helpful.

The KYST program moves the points around in a systematic way so as to make stress smaller and smaller, until further improvement is not possible. Figures 2 and 3 show the end result of this process. The final and smallest stress for the Slavic pseudomap was 0.09 and that of Romance was 0.10. These values are small enough under the circumstances to indicate that the pseudomap reflects the data tolerably well. Interpretation of stress values is a delicate matter that requires considerable study, since stress is influenced by several technical factors (see for example Kruskal and Wish, 1978).

The Slavic pseudomap in Figure 2 displays a phenomenon which has turned out to be common for pseudomaps of dialects: the pseudomap, with the aid of rotation and the other changes mentioned above, corresponds to the geographical map of the speech variabilities fairly well. Figure 4 shows the Slavic pseudomap superimposed on a map of Western Europe. (Little effort was made to find the enlargement factor which would permit the best superimposition.) Each point representing a variety of Non-Slovenian lies reasonably close to the geographical area in which the variety is spoken. Presumably, the historical reason for this is that the diffusion effect tends to decrease with geographical distance, so that the lexicostatistical percentages vary inversely with distance. However, in view of the many factors other than geographical distance which can affect linguistic diffusion, the correspondence shown in Figure 4 seems remarkable. The fact that the point representing Slovenian is not near the area where Slovenian is spoken reflects the classification of Slovenian as a separate *language* coordinate with Non-Slovenian, a matter which is discussed in Section 5.2 and which is based on its lexicostatistical percentages with other Slavic dialects all being below below the language limit of 70%.

The Romance pseudomap in Figure 3 also bears some resemblance to the geographical map, but in this case the resemblance is complicated by historical factors and by geographical factors other than distance. Rome was the original center of dispersal of Romance, and linguistic diffusion

FIGURE 4. Slavic Pseudomap on Geographic Map.

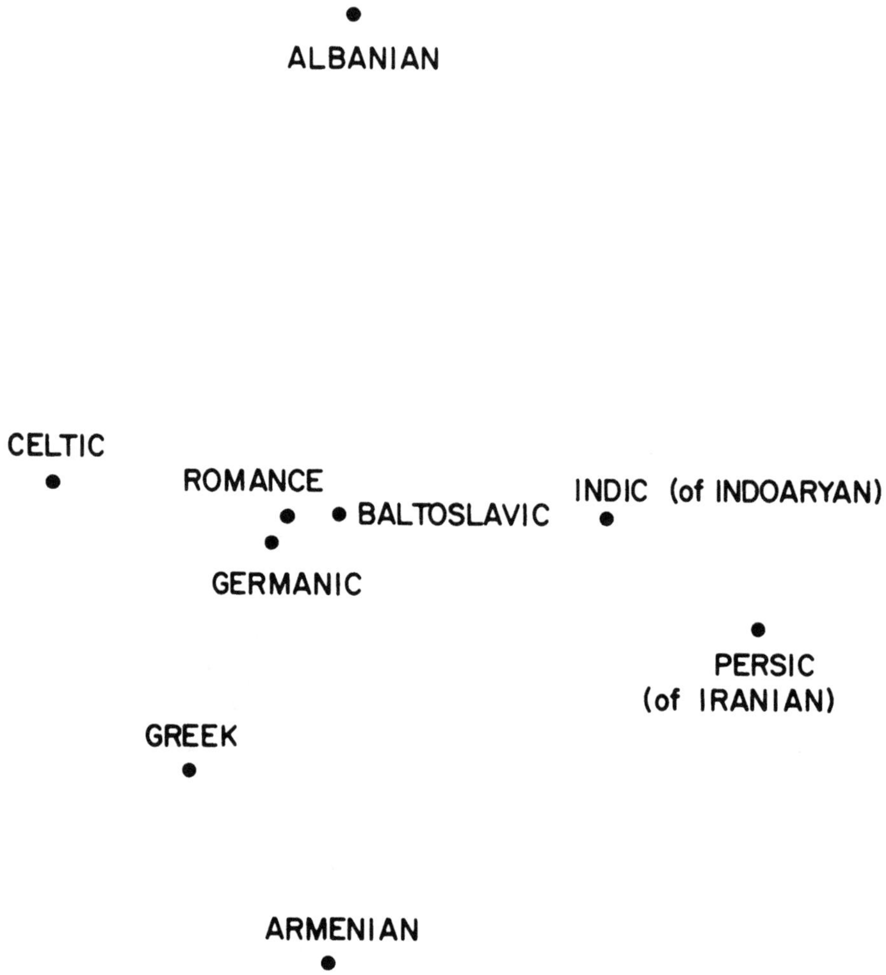

ALBANIAN

CELTIC

ROMANCE

BALTOSLAVIC

INDIC (of INDOARYAN)

GERMANIC

PERSIC
(of IRANIAN)

GREEK

ARMENIAN

FIGURE 5. Pseudomap of Major Indoeuropean Branches.

between geographically noncontiguous varieties was surely limited. The point representing Italian is accordingly central, and peripheral points cluster first into subsets representing geographically contiguous varieties and, as in the case of Brazilian, their recent colonial extensions. The points representing the contiguous Iberian and Franco-Provençal varieties are sufficiently numerous to show a more straightforward geographical ordering. Under the circumstances the Romance pseudomap seems to be as appropriate as any possible alternative, and considerably better than some. For example, a pseudomap which permuted the positions of Italian, Sardinian N, and the pair of **French Creole varieties (if these are treated for the sake of argument as three coordinate subgroups of Western Romance as shown in Figure 1; for the view of **French Creole, see Section 1.3) would appear considerably less appropriate.

The meaningfulness of the pseudomaps both supports the general validity of the percentages within the Slavic Subfamily and within the Romance Subfamily, and confirms the inadequacy of hierarchical classification in these two instances. Any tendency for the Germanic percentages to deviate from a hierarchical pattern probably reflects similar causes, but here analysis is complicated by the fact that Germanic contains three distinct languages: English, Nordic, and Dutch-German. The maximum number of lists available for a single language, namely the seven lists of Nordic, is rather small for applying multidimensional scaling. The relationship among the three languages themselves is at the same time sufficiently hierarchical to complicate an MDS analysis of Germanic as a whole.

When the appearance of one or more language boundaries distributes the varieties of a language among descendant languages, nonhierarchical relationships among varieties of the different descendants can persist with gradually decreasing importance for some time. No doubt this phenomenon is the reason for the well-known fact that *no* hierarchical classification of the major groups of Indoeuropean provides a good explanation of the early Indoeuropean relationships. A multidimensional scaling[7] pseudomap of the nine Indoeuropean groups is presented in

7. This scaling was a metric one, using linear regression with a constant term. The percentages among the groups were averaged, and the averages transformed by an empirically developed transformation so as to yield an approximately straight scatter plot. The transformation used was $(\ln p)^{1.5}$, where p is the averaged percentage value.

Figure 5. Perhaps this reflects some nonhierarchical patterning of the ancient Indoeuropean dialects before they separated into different languages.

8. CONCLUSIONS

The lexicostatistical method has been tested by applying it to the Indoeuropean languages and comparing the results with the generally accepted classification. Since our chief purpose was to test the method as it is applied in other contexts, particularly including the classification of Austronesian languages in LCAL, care was taken to apply it in the same manner used there. Since historical evidence of older languages and migrations is skimpy or entirely absent for most Austronesian languages and for most other language families to which the lexicostatistical method might be applied, we deliberately excluded the use of such information, and used only word lists from contemporary languages. These self-imposed restrictions, which are not intrinsic to lexicostatistics, limited the present classification in a few places.

The resulting lexicostatistical classification of Indoeuropean languages approximates the generally accepted classification. (The differences are fully described in Chapter 5.) The most serious difference is the absence in the present classification of an Indoiranian group. Since the nonlexicostatistical evidence for this group is overwhelming, the difference must result from the failure of the present classification to include it. Of course the chief evidence normally adduced to support this group is based on records of ancient languages which are outside our purview, so the failure can reasonably be attributed to the self-imposed restriction to contemporary languages. Whether or not the traditional method of subgrouping would have discovered this group in the absence of historical records is a matter for speculation. It is not unlikely that the failure of contemporary word lists to support this group is due in part to the effect of intimate borrowing. Such borrowings are to be expected, particularly in the Iranian languages and the languages of northern India, in view of the successive conquests of the area by invaders from the west (Arabic speakers) and north (Mongols). Arabic was the most important source of such borrowings, and in northern India, Iranian was also an important source.

Other differences of note are: (1) a weak indication of a Mesoeuropeic group including Romance (the only modern representative of Italic), Germanic, and Baltoslavic languages, to which perhaps ultimately the Celtic languages are to be added in agreement with Meillet's argument for a northwestern group of Indoeuropean languages; (2) the absence of the generally accepted tripartite division of the Slavic languages into eastern, western, and southern groups; (3) the classification of English as equidistant from Dutch-German and Nordic, the latter two being set closer to each other than to English; and (4) the failure to relate English immediately with Frisian in accordance with the Ingveonic hypothesis. Regarding differences (3) and (4), the generally accepted classifications both depend on historical information outside our purview. As to point (3), there is some uncertainty as to whether English became an independent language before or after the separation of Nordic and Dutch-German into separate languages. Although the traditional treatment, which effectively places the first event after the second, is probably correct, this inference is clearly based on an interpretation of earlier records. As to point (4), evidence for the Ingvȩonic hypothesis includes records that indicate the place of origin of the Germanic invaders of England, and also resemblances and agreements between Frisian and Anglo-Saxon. Although Frisian is probably a separate language from Dutch-German, it is uncertain whether Frisian separated from Dutch-German before or after it separated from English. Only if it separated beforehand would it conform to the Ingveonic hypothesis, so that the lexicostatistical classification may not necessarily be in error in not forming an Ingveonic group. However, the high percentage of Frisian with Dutch possibly indicates at least some undetected intimate borrowing so that the lexicostatistical evidence is not clear on this point. It is important to recognize that nearly all these differences result from rather small percentage point differences.

The lexicostatistical classification supports the Baltoslavic hypothesis strongly and contraindicates the Italoceltic hypothesis (as distinct from the Mesoeuropeic hypothesis formulated above) about as strongly, though Celtic intimate borrowing may have affected the percentages. In the Slavic field Slovenian is rather markedly and almost equally differentiated from all other Slavic speech varieties including Shtokavian Serbocroatian; there remains the possibility that Kajkavian is a transitional dialect or a member of a transitional chain of dialects linking Slovenian with Serbocroatian.

Despite the differences, which catch the eye because they bear on long mooted issues, the widespread agreement between the lexicostatistical classification and widely held views concerning the classification of the members of the Indoeuropean family lends support to the general validity of the lexicostatistical method. The failure of lexicostatistical evidence to support the widely accepted Indoiranian hypothesis in particular reminds us that no type of evidence bearing on linguistic prehistory is completely infallible, or needs to be, and that all evidence, whether arrived at by lexicostatistics or by the traditional method, must be treated with due care. At the same time, the fact that the lexicostatistical evidence also bears strongly on the somewhat controversial Baltoslavic and Italoceltic hypotheses furthermore demonstrates the value of independent lexicostatistical evidence even after extensive comparative reconstruction.

BIBLIOGRAPHY

ABBREVIATIONS

LCAL stands for "Lexicostatistical Classification of the Austronesian Languages," and refers to Dyen (1965).

REFERENCES

V. I. Abaev. 1950. *Russko-Osetinskij Slovar'*. Moscow.

M. R. Anderberg. 1973. *Cluster Analysis for Applications*. New York: Academic Press.

Serban Andronescu. 1961. *Dictionar de Duzunar Englesz-Romîn*. Bucharest.

D. Arzumznov and X. K. Karimov. 1957. *Russko-Tadžikskij Slovar'*. Moscow.

Knut Bergsland and Hans Vogt. 1962. On the validity of glottochronology. *Current Anthropology* 3.115-153.

H. Birnbaum. 1966a. Dialects of common Slavic. Pp. 153-197 in Birnbaum and Puhvel 1966.

Henrik Birnbaum and Jaan Puhvel (eds.) 1966. *Ancient Indo-European Dialects*. Berkeley and Los Angeles.

P. Black. 1976. Multidimensional scaling applied to linguistic relationships. Pp. 43-92 in I. Dyen and G. Jucquois (eds.), *Lexicostatistics in Genetic Linguistics* II; Proceedings of the Montreal Conference, 1973. Cahiers de l'Institut de Linguistique de Louvain, Tome 3.5-6 (1975-1976), December 1976.

Leonard Bloomfield. 1933. *Language*. New York: Holt.

Carl Darling Buck. 1949. *A Dictionary of Selected Synonyms in the Principal Indo-European Languages*. Chicago.

John B. Carroll and I. Dyen. 1962. High-speed computation of lexicostatistical indices. *Language* 38.274-278.

J. D. Carroll and J. B. Kruskal. 1978. Scaling, multidimensional. Pp. 893-907, in W. Kruskal and J. Tanur (eds.), *International Encyclopedia of Statistics*. New York.

C. Douglas Chrétien. 1962. The mathematical models of glottochronology. *Language* 38.11-37.

Warren Cowgill. 1970. Italic and Celtic superlatives and the dialects of Indo-European. Pp. 113-153 in G. Cardona, H. M. Hoenigswald, and A. Senn, *Indo-European and Indo-Europeans*. Philadelphia.

A. Cuyás. 1940. *Appleton's New English-Spanish and Spanish-English Dictionary*. New York.

E. R. Danner. 1951. *Pennsylvania Dutch Dictionary.* York.

R. P. Xavier de Fourvières. 1902. *Lou Pichot Tresor: Dictionnaire Provençal -Français et Français- Provençal.* Avignon.

A. Richard Diebold, Jr. 1964. A control case for glottochronology. *American Anthropologist* 66.987-1006.

A. J. Dobson, J. B. Kruskal, D. Sankoff, and L. J. Savage. 1972. The mathematics of glottochronology revisited. *Anthropological Linguistics* 14.6.205-212.

I. Dyen. 1963. Lexicostatistically determined borrowing and taboo. *Language* 39.60-66.

I. Dyen. 1965. A lexicostatistical classification of the Austronesian languages. *International Journal of American Linguistics*, Memoir 19.

I. Dyen, A. T. James, and J. W. L. Cole. 1967. Language divergence and estimated word retention rate. *Language* 43.150-171.

I. Dyen. 1969. Reconstruction, the comparative method, and the proto-language uniformity assumption. *Language* 45.499-518.

I. Dyen. 1973a. The validity of the mathematical model of glottochronology. Pp. 11-29 in I. Dyen (ed.), *Lexicostatistics in Genetic Linguistics.* The Hague: Mouton.

I. Dyen. 1973b. The impact of lexicostatistics on comparative linguistics. Pp. 75-84 in I. Dyen (ed.), *Lexicostatistics in Genetic Linguistics.* The Hague: Mouton.

I. Dyen. 1975. Creolization in genetic theory. Paper presented at the International Conference on Pidgins and Creoles, January 13-18, 1975. Honolulu. Ms.

I. Dyen and G. Jucquois (eds.) 1976. *Lexicostatistics in Genetic Linguistics* II; Proceedings of the Montreal Conference, 1973. Cahiers de l'Institut de Linguistique de Louvain, Tome 3.5-6 (1975-1976), December 1976.

I. Dyen. 1976. Lexicostatistics: present and prospects. Pp. 5-28 in I. Dyen and G. Jucquois (eds.), *Lexicostatistics in Genetic Linguistics* II. Proceedings of the Montreal Conference, 1973. Cahiers de l'Institut de Linguistique de Louvain, Tome 3.5-6 (1975-1976), December 1976.

I. Fodor. 1961. The validity of glottochronology on the basis of the Slavonic languages. *Studia Slavica* 7.295-346.

G. W. Gilbertson. 1925. *English-Balochi Colloquial Dictionary.* Hertford.

J. Hartigan. 1975. *Clustering Algorithms.* New York: Wiley.

J. Haust. 1948. *Dictionnaire Français- Liègeois.* Liège.

C. Hockett. 1958. *A Course in Modern Linguistics*. New York.

O. Jespersen. 1972. *Growth and Structure of the English Language*. 9th ed. Oxford.

S. C. Johnson. 1967. Hierarchical clustering schemes. *Psychometrika* 32.241-254.

M. Joos. 1964. Glottochronology with retention-rate inhomogeneity (Abstract). P. 237 in H. Lunt (ed.) *Proceedings of the Ninth International Congress of Linguists*. The Hague: Mouton.

K. Karre et al. 1935. *English-Swedish Dictionary*. Stockholm.

T. Kriel. 1945. *Die Nuwe Afrikaanse Skool-Wordenboek*. Kaapstad.

J. B. Kruskal. 1972. (2nd ed., 1978). The meaning of words. Pp. 185-194 in Tanur et al. (eds.), *Statistics: A Guide to the Unknown*. San Francisco: Holden-Day.

J. B. Kruskal. 1977. Multidimensional scaling and other methods for discovering structure. Pp. 296-339 in Enslein, Ralston, and Wilf (eds.), *Statistical Methods for Digital Computers*. (Volume III of Mathematical Methods for Digitial Computers.) New York: Wiley.

J. B. Kruskal, I. Dyen, and P. Black. 1971. The vocabulary method of reconstructing language trees: innovations and large-scale applications. Pp. 361-380 in Kendall and Tautu · (eds.), *Mathematics in the Archeological and Historical Sciences*. Edinburgh University Press: Edinburgh.

J. B. Kruskal, I. Dyen, and P. Black. 1973. Some results from the vocabulary method of reconstructing language trees. Pp. 30-55 in I. Dyen (ed.), *Lexicostatistics in Genetic Linguistics*. The Hague: Mouton.

J. B. Kruskal and M. Wish. 1978. *Multidimensional Scaling*. Sage University Papers 07-011. Beverly Hills and London.

T. O. Lane. 1904. *Lane's English-Irish Dictionary*. Dublin.

H. Lima and G. Barroso. 1949. *Pequenho Dicionário Brasileiro da Lingua Portuguesa*. Rio de Janeiro.

D. L. R. Lorimer. 1958. *The Wakhi Language*. London.

John Gordon Lorimer. 1902. *Grammar and Vocabulary of Waziri Pashto*. Calcutta.

F. Lounsbury. 1961. *Iroquois-Cherokee linguistics relations*. Bureau of American Ethnology Bulletin 180.9-17.

G. H. Lunt. 1952. *A Grammar of the Macedonian Literary Language*. Skopje.

A. Meillet. 1922. *Les Dialectes Indo-européens*. Paris.

A. Meillet and M. Cohen. 1952. *Les Langues du Monde*. Paris.

H. Michaelis. 1893. *A New Dictionary of the Portuguese and English Languages*. London.

G. W. P. Money. 1942. *Gurkali Manual*. Bombay.

L'Abbé Olinger. 1852. *Nouveau Dictionnaire de Poche Français-Flamand*. Malines.

José Pujal y Serra. 1911. *Diccionario Catalán-Castellano*. Barcelona.

M. Reno. 1943. *Portuguese: A Handbook of Brazilian Conversation*. Chicago.

David Sankoff. 1969. Historical linguistics as stochastic process. Ph.D. thesis (McGill U.).

A. Schleicher. 1861. (2nd ed., 1876). *Compendium der vergleichenden Grammatik der indogermanischen Sprachen*. Weimar.

Alfred Senn. 1966. The relationships of Baltic and Slavic. Pp. 139-151 in Birnbaum and Puhvel.

P. A. Sneath and R. R. Sokal. 1973. *Numerical Taxonomy*. San Francisco: W. H. Freeman.

M. Swadesh. 1952. Lexico-statistic dating of prehistoric ethnic contacts: with special reference to North American Indians and Eskimos. *Proceedings of the American Philosphical Society* 96.452-463.

D. C. Swanson. 1959. *Vocabulary of Modern Spoken Greek*. Minneapolis.

J. Tischler. 1973. *Glottochronologie und Lexikostatistik*. Innsbruck.

R. L. Turner. 1931. *A Comparative and Etymological Dictionary of the Nepali Language*. London.

F. Vallée. 1919. *Vocabulaire Français-Breton*. St.-Brienc.

N. Van der Merwe. 1966. New mathematics for glottochronology. *Current Anthropology* 7.485-500.

J. Van Ryzin (ed.) 1977. *Classification and Clustering*. New York: Academic Press.

N. Van Wijk. 1956. *Les Langues Slaves: de l'Unité à la Pluralité*. 's-Gravenhage.

Ant. Velleman. 1929. *Dicziunari Scurzieu de la lingua Ladina*. Samaden.

C. F. and F. M. Voegelin. 1977. *Classification and Index of the World's Languages*. New York.

Calvert Watkins. 1966. Italo-Celtic revisited. Pp. 29-50 in Birnbaum and Puhvel.

G. Weigand. 1914. *Albanesisch-Deutsches, Deutsch-Albanesisches Wörterbuch*. Leipzig.

H. R. Wullschlägel. 1856. *Deutsch-Negerenglisches Wörterbuch*. Löbau.

P. B. Zudin. 1955. *Russko-Afganskij Slovar'*. Moscow.

A1. THE CLASSIFICATION IN OUTLINE FORM

• A heavy dot below indicates a *list* as opposed to a *group*.
** For the meaning of double asterisks below, see Sections 2.3 and 2.4.

Indoeuropean Family.

1. 1. Celtic Subfamily 18.3 (2. Mesoeuropeic Hesion: 2.1. Romance Subfamily).
1.1. 1.1. Irish [Subfamily] 33.5 (1.2. Brythonic Subfamily).
1.1.1• 1.1.1• Irish A 82.6 (1.1.2• Irish B).
1.1.2• 1.1.2• Irish B 82.6 (1.1.1• Irish A).
1.2. 1.2. Brythonic Subfamily 33.5 (1.1. Irish).
1.2.1. 1.2.1. Welsh [Subfamily] 62.5 (1.2.2. Breton).
1.2.1.1• 1.2.1.1• Welsh N 93.9 (1.2.1.2• Welsh C).
1.2.1.2• 1.2.1.2• Welsh C 93.9 (1.2.1.1• Welsh N).
1.2.2. 1.2.2. Breton [Subfamily] 62.5 (1.2.1. Welsh).
1.2.2.1• 1.2.2.1• Breton List 92.9 (1.2.2.3• Breton ST).
1.2.2.2• 1.2.2.2• Breton SE 94.9 (1.2.2.3• Breton ST).
1.2.2.3• 1.2.2.3• Breton ST 94.9 (1.2.2.2• Breton SE), 92.9 (1.2.2.1• Breton List).

2. 2. Mesoeuropeic Hesion: 2.3. Baltoslavic Subfamily 18.6 (3. Indoaryan Cluster: 3.3. Indic Subfamily), 13.5 (7. **Albanian); 2.1. Romance Subfamily 18.3 (1. Celtic Subfamily); 2.2. Germanic Subfamily 17.1 (4. Greek).

2.1. 2.1. Romance Subfamily 23.5 (2.2. Germanic Subfamily).

2.1.1. 2.1.1. Rumanian [Subfamily] 56.8 (2.1.2. Western Romance Subfamily).

2.1.1.1• 2.1.1.1• Rumanian List 72.3 (2.1.1.2• Vlach).

2.1.1.2• 2.1.1.2• Vlach 72.3 (2.1.1.1• Rumanian List).

2.1.2. 2.1.2. Western Romance Subfamily 56.8 (2.1.1. Rumanian).

2.1.2.1• 2.1.2.1• Italian 83.2 (2.1.2.2• Ladin), 81.8 (2.1.2.3. Franco-Provençal Cluster: 2.1.2.3.1• Provençal), 79.7 (2.1.2.6. Western Sardinian Hesion: 2.1.2.6.1• Sardinian L), 78.4 (2.1.2.7. Iberian), 76.4 (2.1.2.8• Catalan).

2.1.2.2• 2.1.2.2• Ladin 83.2 (2.1.2.1• Italian).

2.1.2.3. 2.1.2.3. Franco-Provençal Cluster: 2.1.2.3.2• French 83.6 (2.1.2.4. **French Creole); 2.1.2.3.1• Provençal 81.8 (2.1.2.1• Italian).

2.1.2.3.1• 2.1.2.3.1• Provençal 89.9 (2.1.2.3.2• French).

2.1.2.3.2• 2.1.2.3.2• French 89.9 (2.1.2.3.1• Provençal), 89.4 (2.1.2.3.3• Walloon).

2.1.2.3.3• 2.1.2.3.3• Walloon 89.4 (2.1.2.3.2• French).

2.1.2.4. 2.1.2.4. **French Creole [Subfamily] 83.6 (2.1.2.3. Franco-Provençal Cluster: 2.1.2.3.2• French).

2.1.2.4.1• 2.1.2.4.1• **French Creole C 97.4 (2.1.2.4.2• **French Creole D).

2.1.2.4.2• 2.1.2.4.2• **French Creole D 97.4 (2.1.2.4.1• **French Creole C).

2.1.2.5• 2.1.2.5• Sardinian N 79.6 (2.1.2.6. Western Sardinian Hesion: 2.1.2.6.1• Sardinian L).

2.1.2.6. 2.1.2.6. Western Sardinian Hesion: 2.1.2.6.1• Sardinian L 79.7 (2.1.2.1• Italian), 79.6 (2.1.2.5• Sardinian N).

2.1.2.6.1• 2.1.2.6.1• Sardinian L 83.2 (2.1.2.6.2• Sardinian C).

2.1.2.6.2• 2.1.2.6.2• Sardinian C 83.2 (2.1.2.6.1• Sardinian L)

2.1.2.7. 2.1.2.7. Iberian [Genus] 78.4 (2.1.2.1• Italian).

2.1.2.7.1• 2.1.2.7.1• Spanish 86.8 (2.1.2.7.2. Portuguese).

2.1.2.7.2. 2.1.2.7.2. Portuguese [Subfamily] 86.8 (2.1.2.7.1• Spanish).

2.1.2.7.2.1• 2.1.2.7.2.1• Portuguese ST 96.9 (2.1.2.7.2.2• Brazilian).

2.1.2.7.2.2• 2.1.2.7.2.2• Brazilian 96.9 (2.1.2.7.2.1• Portuguese ST).

2.1.2.8• 2.1.2.8• Catalan 76.4 (2.1.2.1• Italian).

2.2.	2.2. Germanic Subfamily 23.5 (2.1. Romance Subfamily), 22.2 (2.3. Baltoslavic Subfamily).
2.2.1.	2.2.1. Continental Germanic Hesion: 2.2.1.1. Dutch-German 57.3 (2.2.2.1• English ST).
2.2.1.1.	2.2.1.1. Dutch-German [Subfamily] 61.6 (2.2.1.2. Nordic).
2.2.1.1.1•	2.2.1.1.1• German ST 85.8 (2.2.1.1.2• Pennsylvania Dutch), 84.0 (2.2.1.1.3. Dutch).
2.2.1.1.2•	2.2.1.1.2• Pennsylvania Dutch 85.8 (2.2.1.1.1• German ST)
2.2.1.1.3.	2.2.1.1.3. Dutch [Subfamily] 84.0 (2.2.1.1.1• German ST), 82.2 (2.2.1.1.4• Frisian).
2.2.1.1.3.1•	2.2.1.1.3.1• Dutch List 96.5 (2.2.1.1.3.2• Afrikaans).
2.2.1.1.3.2•	2.2.1.1.3.2• Afrikaans 97.0 (2.2.1.1.3.3• Flemish), 96.5 (2.2.1.1.3.1• Dutch List).
2.2.1.1.3.3•	2.2.1.1.3.3• Flemish 97.0 (2.2.1.1.3.2• Afrikaans).
2.2.1.1.4•	2.2.1.1.4• Frisian 82.2 (2.2.1.1.3. Dutch).
2.2.1.2.	2.2.1.2. Nordic [Subfamily] 61.6 (2.2.1.1. Dutch-German).
2.2.1.2.1.	2.2.1.2.1. Scandinavian Cluster: 2.2.1.2.1.1. Swedish Hesion 2.2.1.2.1.1.1• Swedish Up 80.6 (2.2.1.2.2. Icelandic).
2.2.1.2.1.1.	2.2.1.2.1.1. Swedish Hesion: 2.2.1.2.1.1.3• Swedish List 87.4 (2.2.1.2.1.2• Danish)
2.2.1.2.1.1.1•	2.2.1.2.1.1.1• Swedish Up 92.5 (2.2.1.2.1.1.2• Swedi VL), 91.0 (2.2.1.2.1.1.3• Swedish List).
2.2.1.2.1.1.2•	2.2.1.2.1.1.2• Swedish VL 92.5 (2.2.1.2.1.1.1• Swedish Up).
2.2.1.2.1.1.3•	2.2.1.2.1.1.3• Swedish List 91.0 (2.2.1.2.1.1.1• Swedish Up).
2.2.1.2.1.2•	2.2.1.2.1.2• Danish 87.4 (2.2.1.2.1.1. Swedish Hesion: 2.2.1.2.1.1.3• Swedish List), 85.4 (2.2.1.2.1.3• Riksmal).
2.2.1.2.1.3•	2.2.1.2.1.3• Riksmal 85.4 (2.2.1.2.1.2• Danish).
2.2.1.2.2.	2.2.1.2.2. Icelandic [Subfamily] 80.6 (2.2.1.2.1. Scandinavian Cluster: 2.2.1.2.1.1. Swedish Hesion: 2.2.1.2.1.1.1• Swedish Up).
2.2.1.2.2.1•	2.2.1.2.2.1• Icelandic ST 92.2 (2.2.1.2.2.2• Faroese).
2.2.1.2.2.2•	2.2.1.2.2.2• Faroese 92.2 (2.2.1.2.2.1• Icelandic ST).
2.2.2.	2.2.2. English 57.3 (2.2.1. Continental Germanic Hesion: 2.2.1.1. Dutch-German).
2.2.2.1•	2.2.2.1• English ST 65.8 (2.2.2.2• **Takitaki).
2.2.2.2•	2.2.2.2• **Takitaki 65.8 (2.2.2.1• English ST).

2.3. 2.3. Baltoslavic Subfamily 22.2 (2.2. Germanic Subfamily).
2.3.1. 2.3.1. Baltic Subfamily 34.2 (2.3.2. Slavic Subfamily).
2.3.1.1. 2.3.1.1. Lithuanian [Subfamily] 58.7 (2.3.1.2• Latvian).
2.3.1.1.1• 2.3.1.1.1• Lithuanian O 89.9 (2.3.1.1.2• Lithuanian ST).
2.3.1.1.2• 2.3.1.1.2• Lithuanian ST 89.9 (2.3.1.1.1• Lithuanian O).
2.3.1.2• 2.3.1.2• Latvian 58.7 (2.3.1.1. Lithuanian).

2.3.2.	2.3.2. Slavic Subfamily 34.2 (2.3.1. Baltic Subfamily).
2.3.2.1•	2.3.2.1• Slovenian 65.6 (2.3.2.2. Non-Slovenian Slavic).
2.3.2.2.	2.3.2.2. Non-Slovenian Slavic [Subfamily] 65.6 (2.3.2.1• Slovenian).
2.3.2.2.1.	2.3.2.2.1. Lusatian [Subfamily] 82.2 (2.3.2.2.2. Czechoslovakian Cluster: 2.3.2.2.2.1. Czechoslovak Hesion: 2.3.2.2.2.1.1• Czech), 79.5 (2.3.2.2.6. South Slavic Hesion: 2.3.2.2.6.1• Macedonian).
2.3.2.2.1.1•	2.3.2.2.1.1• Lusatian L 95.8 (2.3.2.2.1.2• Lusatian U).
2.3.2.2.1.2•	2.3.2.2.1.2• Lusatian U 95.8 (2.3.2.2.1.1• Lusatian L).
2.3.2.2.2.	2.3.2.2.2. Czechoslovakian Cluster: 2.3.2.2.2.1. Czechoslovak Hesion: 2.3.2.2.2.1.1• Czech 82.2 (2.3.2.2.1. Lusatian); 2.3.2.2.2.1. Czechoslovak Hesion: 2.3.2.2.2.1.2• Slovak 81.3 (2.3.2.2.3. East Central Slavic Hesion: 2.3.2.2.3.1• Ukrainian).
2.3.2.2.2.1.	2.3.2.2.2.1. Czechoslovak Hesion: 2.3.2.2.2.1.1• Czech 88.3 (2.3.2.2.2.2• Czech E).
2.3.2.2.2.1.1•	2.3.2.2.2.1.1• Czech 91.4 (2.3.2.2.2.1.2• Slovak).
2.3.2.2.2.1.2•	2.3.2.2.2.1.2• Slovak 91.4 (2.3.2.2.2.1.1• Czech).
2.3.2.2.2.2•	2.3.2.2.2.2• Czech E 88.3 (2.3.2.2.2.1. Czechoslovak Hesion: 2.3.2.2.2.1.1• Czech).
2.3.2.2.3.	2.3.2.2.3. East Central Slavic Hesion: 2.3.2.2.3.1• Ukrainian (2.3.2.2.2. Czechoslovakian Cluster: 2.3.2.2.2.1. Czechoslovak Hesion: 2.3.2.2.2.1.2• Slovak), 80.2 (2.3.2.2.4• Polish), 77.9 (2.3.2.2.5• Russian).
2.3.2.2.3.1•	2.3.2.2.3.1• Ukrainian 83.9 (2.3.2.2.3.2• Byelorussian).
2.3.2.2.3.2•	2.3.2.2.3.2• Byelorussian 83.9 (2.3.2.2.3.1• Ukrainian).
2.3.2.2.4•	2.3.2.2.4• Polish 80.2 (2.3.2.2.3. East Central Slavic Hesion: 2.3.2.2.3.1• Ukrainian).
2.3.2.2.5•	2.3.2.2.5• Russian 77.9 (2.3.2.2.3. East Central Slavic Hesion: 2.3.2.2.3.1• Ukrainian).
2.3.2.2.6.	2.3.2.2.6. South Slavic Hesion: 2.3.2.2.6.1• Macedonian 79.5 (2.3.2.2.1. Lusatian).
2.3.2.2.6.1•	2.3.2.2.6.1• Macedonian 83.5 (2.3.2.2.6.2• Bulgarian), 82.5 (2.3.2.2.6.3• Serbocroatian).
2.3.2.2.6.2•	2.3.2.2.6.2• Bulgarian 83.5 (2.3.2.2.6.1• Macedonian).
2.3.2.2.6.3•	2.3.2.2.6.3• Serbocroatian 82.5 (2.3.2.2.6.1• Macedonian).

3. 3. Indoaryan Cluster: 3.3. Indic Subfamily 18.6 (2. Mesoeuropeic Hesion: 2.3 Baltoslavic Subfamily), 18.1 (6. Iranian Cluster: 6.2. East Iranian Hesion: 6.2.2. Persic Subfamily).

3.1• 3.1• Gypsy Gk 27.5 (3.3. Indic Subfamily).

3.2• 3.2• Singhalese 25.3 (3.3. Indic Subfamily).

3.3. 3.3. Indic Subfamily 27.5 (3.1• Gypsy Gk), 25.3 (3.2• Singhalese).

3.3.1• 3.3.1• Kashmiri 40.1 (3.3.2. Sindhic Subfamily).

3.3.2. 3.3.2. Sindhic Subfamily 40.1 (3.3.1• Kashmiri).

3.3.2.1. 3.3.2.1. Gangetic Hesion: 3.3.2.1.3• Bengali 51.1 (3.3.2.2. Nepali).

3.3.2.1.1. 3.3.2.1.1. Marathic Cluster: 3.3.2.1.1.2• Gujarati 55.2 (3.3.2.1.2. Hindic); 3.3.2.1.1.1• Marathi 55.0 (3.3.2.1.3• Bengali).

3.3.2.1.1.1• 3.3.2.1.1.1• Marathi 61.3 (3.3.2.1.1.2• Gujarati).

3.3.2.1.1.2• 3.3.2.1.1.2• Gujarati 61.3 (3.3.2.1.1.1• Marathi).

3.3.2.1.2. 3.3.2.1.2. Hindic [Subfamily] 55.2 (3.3.2.1.1. Marathic Cluster: 3.3.2.1.1.2• Gujarati).

3.3.2.1.2.1. 3.3.2.1.2.1. Panjabi Hesion: 3.3.2.1.2.1.1• Panjabi ST 74.5 (3.3.2.1.2.2• **Hindi).

3.3.2.1.2.1.1• 3.3.2.1.2.1.1• Panjabi ST 77.0 (3.3.2.1.2.1.2• Lahnda).

3.3.2.1.2.1.2• 3.3.2.1.2.1.2• Lahnda 77.0 (3.3.2.1.2.1.1• Panjabi ST).

3.3.2.1.2.2• 3.3.2.1.2.2• **Hindi 74.5 (3.3.2.1.2.1. Panjabi Hesion: 3.3.2.1.2.1.1• Panjabi ST).

3.3.2.1.3• 3.3.2.1.3• Bengali 55.0 (3.3.2.1.1. Marathic Cluster: 3.3.2.1.1.1• Marathi).

3.3.2.2. 3.3.2.2. Nepali [Subfamily] 51.1 (3.3.2.1. Gangetic Hesion: 3.3.2.1.3• Bengali).

3.3.2.2.1• 3.3.2.2.1• **Nepali List 85.2 (3.3.2.2.2• Khaskura).

3.3.2.2.2• 3.3.2.2.2• Khaskura 85.2 (3.3.2.2.1• **Nepali List).

4. 4. Greek [Subfamily] 17.1 (2. Mesoeuropeic Hesion: 2.2. Germanic Subfamily), 17.0 (5. Armenian).

4.1. 4.1. Demotic Greek [Subfamily] 69.9 (4.2• **Greek K).

4.1.1• 4.1.1• Greek ML 92.3 (4.1.2• Greek MD).

4.1.2• 4.1.2• Greek MD 92.3 (4.1.1• Greek ML), 91.8 (4.1.3• Greek Mod), 90.7 (4.1.4• Greek D).

4.1.3• 4.1.3• Greek Mod 91.8 (4.1.2• Greek MD).

4.1.4• 4.1.4• Greek D 90.7 (4.1.2• Greek MD).

4.2• 4.2• **Greek K 69.9 (4.1. Demotic Greek).

5.	5. Armenian [Subfamily] 17.0 (4. Greek).
5.1•	5.1• Armenian Mod 72.2 (5.2• Armenian List).
5.2•	5.2• Armenian List 72.2 (5.1• Armenian Mod).
6.	6. Iranian Cluster: 6.2. East Iranian Hesion: 6.2.2. Persic Subfamily 18.1 (3. Indoaryan Cluster: 3.3. Indic Subfamily).
6.1•	6.1• Ossetic 24.5 (6.2. East Iranian Hesion: 6.2.2. Persic Subfamily).
6.2.	6.2. East Iranian Hesion: 6.2.2. Persic Subfamily 24.5 (6.1• Ossetic).
6.2.1.	6.2.1. Afghanic [Subfamily] 27.3 (6.2.2. Persic Subfamily).
6.2.1.1•	6.2.1.1• Afghan 74.9 (6.2.1.2• Waziri).
6.2.1.2•	6.2.1.2• Waziri 74.9 (6.2.1.1• Afghan).
6.2.2.	6.2.2. Persic Subfamily 27.3 (6.2.1. Afghanic).
6.2.2.1.	6.2.2.1. Persian [Subfamily] 45.2 (6.2.2.2• Baluchi), 42.2 (6.2.2.3• Wakhi).
6.2.2.1.1•	6.2.2.1.1• Persian List 81.5 (6.2.2.1.2• Tadžik).
6.2.2.1.2•	6.2.2.1.2• Tadžik 81.5 (6.2.2.1.1• Persian List).
6.2.2.2•	6.2.2.2• Baluchi 45.2 (6.2.2.1. Persian).
6.2.2.3•	6.2.2.3• Wakhi 42.2 (6.2.2.1. Persian).
7.	7. **Albanian [Subfamily] 13.5 (2. Mesoeuropeic Hesion: 2.3. Baltoslavic Subfamily).
7.1.	7.1. Nuclear Albanian [Subfamily] 72.6 (7.2• Albanian K), 71.1 (7.3• Albanian C).
7.1.1.	7.1.1. Tosk Hesion: 7.1.1.1• Albanian T 84.0 (7.1.2• Albanian G).
7.1.1.1•	7.1.1.1• Albanian T 87.9 (7.1.1.2• Albanian Top).
7.1.1.2•	7.1.1.2• Albanian Top 87.9 (7.1.1.1• Albanian T).
7.1.2•	7.1.2• Albanian G 84.0 (7.1.1. Tosk Hesion: 7.1.1.1• Albanian T).
7.2•	7.2• Albanian K 72.6 (7.1. Nuclear Albanian).
7.3•	7.3• Albanian C 71.1 (7.1. Nuclear Albanian).

A2. THE GROUPS AND SPEECH VARIETIES

The listing is in alphabetical order.

• A heavy dot below indicates a *list* as opposed to a *group*.

** For the meaning of double asterisks below, see Sections 2.3 and 2.4.

Number in Outline Classification	*Name or Abbreviation used in Box Diagram*
6.2.1.1•	Afghan
6.2.1.	Afghanic [Subfamily]
2.2.1.1.3.2•	Afrikaans
7.3•	Albanian C
7.1.2•	Albanian G
7.2•	Albanian K
7.1.1.1•	Albanian T
7.1.1.2•	Albanian Top
7.	**Albanian [Subfamily]
7.1.	Albanian, Nuclear = Nuclear Albanian [Subfamily]
5.2•	Armenian List
5.1•	Armenian Mod
5.	Armenian [Subfamily]
2.3.1.	Baltic Subfamily
2.3.	Baltoslavic Subfamily
6.2.2.2•	Baluchi
3.3.2.1.3•	Bengali
2.1.2.7.2.2•	Brazilian
1.2.2.1•	Breton List
1.2.2.2•	Breton SE
1.2.2.3•	Breton ST
1.2.2.	Breton [Subfamily]
1.2.	Brythonic Subfamily
2.3.2.2.6.2•	Bulgarian
2.3.2.2.3.2•	Byelorussian
2.1.2.8•	Catalan
1.	Celtic Subfamily
2.2.1.	CG = Continental Germanic Hesion
2.2.1.	Continental Germanic Hesion
2.1.2.4.	**Creole = **French Creole [Subfamily]
2.1.2.4.1•	**Creole C = **French Creole C
2.1.2.4.2•	**Creole D = **French Creole D
2.3.2.2.2.1.1•	Czech
2.3.2.2.2.2•	Czech E

2.3.2.2.2.1.	Czechoslovak Hesion
2.3.2.2.2.	Czechoslovakian Cluster
2.2.1.2.1.2.	Danish
4.1.	Demotic Greek [Subfamily]
2.2.1.1.3.1.	Dutch List
2.2.1.1.3.	Dutch [Subfamily]
2.2.1.1.	Dutch-German [Subfamily]
2.3.2.2.3.	East Central Slavic Hesion
6.2.	East Iranian Hesion
2.3.2.2.3.	ECS = East Central Slavic Hesion
2.2.2.	English
2.2.2.1.	English ST
2.2.1.2.2.2.	Faroese
2.2.1.1.3.3.	Flemish
2.1.2.3.	Franco-Provençal Cluster
2.1.2.3.2.	French
2.1.2.4.1.	**French Creole C
2.1.2.4.2.	**French Creole D
2.1.2.4.	**French Creole [Subfamily]
2.2.1.1.4.	Frisian
3.3.2.1.	Gangetic Hesion
2.2.1.1.1.	German ST
2.2.	Germanic Subfamily
2.2.1.	Germanic, Continental = Continental Germanic Hesion
4.1.4.	Greek D
4.2.	**Greek K
4.1.2.	Greek MD
4.1.1.	Greek ML
4.1.3.	Greek Mod
4.	Greek [Subfamily]
4.1.	Greek, Demotic = Demotic Greek [Subfamily]
3.3.2.1.1.2.	Gujarati
3.1.	Gypsy Gk
3.3.2.1.2.2.	**Hindi
3.3.2.1.2.	Hindic [Subfamily]
2.1.2.7.	Iberian [Genus]
2.2.1.2.2.1.	Icelandic ST
2.2.1.2.2.	Icelandic [Subfamily]
3.3.	Indic Subfamily
3.	Indoaryan Cluster
	Indoeuropean Family
6.	Iranian Cluster

6.2.	Iranian, East = East Iranian Hesion
1.1.1•	Irish A
1.1.2•	Irish B
1.1.	Irish [Subfamily]
2.1.2.1•	Italian
3.3.1•	Kashmiri
3.3.2.2.2•	Khaskura
2.1.2.2•	Ladin
3.3.2.1.2.1.2•	Lahnda
2.3.1.2•	Latvian
2.3.1.1.1•	Lithuanian O
2.3.1.1.2•	Lithuanian ST
2.3.1.1.	Lithuanian [Subfamily]
2.3.2.2.1.1•	Lusatian L
2.3.2.2.1.2•	Lusatian U
2.3.2.2.1.	Lusatian [Subfamily]
3.3.2.1.1.	M = Marathic Cluster
2.3.2.2.6.1•	Macedonian
3.3.2.1.1.1•	Marathi
3.3.2.1.1.	Marathic Cluster
2.	Mesoeuropeic Hesion
7.1.	NA = Nuclear Albanian [Subfamily]
3.3.2.2.1•	**Nepali List
3.3.2.2.	Nepali [Subfamily]
2.3.2.2.	Non-Slovenian Slavic [Subfamily]
2.2.1.2.	Nordic [Subfamily]
2.2.1.2.1.3•	[Norwegian] Riksmal = Riksmal
2.3.2.2.	NS = Non-Slovenian Slavic [Subfamily]
7.1.	Nuclear Albanian [Subfamily]
6.1•	Ossetic
2.1.2.7.2.	P = Portuguese [Subfamily]
3.3.2.1.2.1.1•	Panjabi ST
3.3.2.1.2.1.	Panjabi Hesion
2.2.1.1.2•	Pennsylvania Dutch
6.2.2.1.1•	Persian List
6.2.2.1.	Persian [Subfamily]
6.2.2.	Persic Subfamily
2.3.2.2.4•	Polish
2.1.2.7.2.1•	Portuguese ST
2.1.2.7.2.	Portuguese [Subfamily]
2.1.2.3.1•	Provençal
2.2.1.2.1.3•	Riksmal

2.1. Romance Subfamily
2.1.2. Romance, Western = Western Romance Subfamily
2.1.1.1. Rumanian List
2.1.1. Rumanian [Subfamily]
2.3.2.2.5. Russian
2.1.2.6.2. Sardinian C
2.1.2.6.1. Sardinian L
2.1.2.5. Sardinian N
2.1.2.6. Sardinian, Western = Western Sardinian Hesion
2.2.1.2.1. Scandinavian Cluster
2.2.1.2.1. Scv = Scandinavian Cluster
2.3.2.2.6.3. Serbocroatian
3.3.2. Sindhic Subfamily
3.2. Singhalese
2.3.2. Slavic Subfamily
2.3.2.2.3. Slavic, East Central = East Central Slavic Hesion
2.3.2.2. Slavic, Non-Slovenian = Non-Slovenian Slavic [Subfam
2.3.2.2.6. Slavic, South = South Slavic Hesion
2.3.2.2.2.1.2. Slovak
2.3.2.1. Slovenian
2.3.2.2.6. South Slavic Hesion
2.1.2.7.1. Spanish
2.3.2.2.6. SS = South Slavic Hesion
2.2.1.2.1.1.3. Swedish List
2.2.1.2.1.1.1. Swedish Up
2.2.1.2.1.1.2. Swedish VL
2.2.1.2.1.1. Swedish Hesion
6.2.2.1.2. Tadžik
2.2.2.2. **Takitaki
7.1.1. Tosk Hesion
2.3.2.2.3.1. Ukrainian
2.1.1.2. Vlach
6.2.2.3. Wakhi
2.1.2.3.3. Walloon
6.2.1.2. Waziri
1.2.1.2. Welsh C
1.2.1.1. Welsh N
1.2.1. Welsh [Subfamily]
2.1.2. Western Romance Subfamily
2.1.2.6. Western Sardinian Hesion
2.1.2. WR = Western Romance Subfamily
2.1.2.6. WS = Western Sardinian Hesion

A3. THE LEXICOSTATISTICAL METHOD

The lexicostatistical method was invented by Swadesh (1952). This appendix gives a brief description of the lexicostatistical method and of glottochronology. Both are based on lexicostatistical percentages, but the lexicostatistical method means using these percentages to classify the speech varieties, while glottochronology (not used in this work) means using these percentages to assign dates to language splits. Further information may be found in Dyen and Jucquois (1976), in Dyen (1965), and in Kruskal, Dyen, and Black (1971,1973).

The lexicostatistical method starts with a list of M meanings that are so basic that almost every culture has words for them. Swadesh devised a list with $M = 100$ such words, which he later modified and supplemented to make a list with $M = 200$ words. The larger list is used in this work. The English words for a few of the meanings on this list are 'mother', 'father' (but *not* 'brother', 'sister'), 'one', 'two', ... , 'five', 'blood', 'to breathe', 'straight' and 'all'. Phase 1 of lexicostatistics is to collect the forms (i.e., phonetic representations) for the words with these meanings in a group of speech varieties that are already known to belong to a single language family. Phase 2 is performed by a linguist who is knowledgeable about the language family. The linguist works with the meanings one by one. For each meaning, the linguist considers all the forms, and makes expert judgments of cognation among them. The fact that cognation is judged only for forms having the same meaning greatly reduces the probability of erroneous apparent cognation due to chance resemblance, and makes an important contribution to the accuracy of the method.

Two forms are cognate if they have both descended in unbroken lines from the same ancestor. Descent does not include borrowing from one speech variety to another. For example, English 'flower' is not cognate to French 'fleur', because 'flower' was borrowed from the French word. Even in the absence of historical knowledge, this lack of cognation would be recognized because the two forms are not related by the regular phonetic changes which connect English and French. On the other hand, the English word 'blossom' is cognate to 'fleur', and these two words are related by the regular phonetic changes.

Phase 3 of lexicostatistics is to consider each each pair of speech varieties in turn and compute a lexicostatistical percentage between them. To see what this percentage means, consider for example German and

Spanish. In principle, a list is made of the meanings, the German and Spanish words for the meanings, and the cognation decisions, as shown here:

Meaning	German word	Spanish word	Cognation
all	alle	todo	no
and	und	y	no
animal	Tier	animal	no
ashes	Asche	ceniza	no
...	...	...	...
fat	fett	grasa	no
father	Vater	padre	yes
to fear	fürchten	temer	no
...	...	...	...
I	ich	yo	yes
ice	Eis	hielo	no
if	wenn	si	no
...	...	...	...

The percentage of all meanings, i.e., rows, for which the forms are cognate is the lexicostatistical percentage, 25.3%, connecting German and Spanish. Complications occur when a speech variety uses two or more forms for a single meaning, and when cognation is judged indeterminate because the evidence does not support a clear decision. For a discussion of how such complications have been handled, see LCAL.

The lexicostatistical percentage is a measure of similarity. By way of illustration, for the Swadesh list of 200 meanings, dialects of a single language are usually connected by a percentage above 70%. German and English are connected by 57.8%, while French and English are connected by 23.6%.

Phase 4 of lexicostatistics is to subgroup (i.e., classify) the speech varieties into a family tree by some method that is systematic and reasonable but is not specified in detail. Section 2.1 describes the method used in this monograph and how it relates to some other well-known methods. Appendix 6 describes the other well-known methods. All the methods referred to are based on the table described in the remainder of this appendix.

The lexicostatistical percentages can be arranged into a square symmetric table with as many rows and columns as there are speech varieties. Using only the seven Celtic speech varieties, the table is shown here.

		Iri sh A	Iri sh B	Wel sh N	Wel sh C	Bre ton Lst	Bre ton SE	Bre ton ST
1.1.1.	Irish A	0	826	344	342	311	309	319
1.1.2.	Irish B	826	0	355	360	335	321	328
1.2.1.1.	Welsh N	344	355	0	939	639	629	641
1.2.1.2.	Welsh C	342	360	939	0	615	610	617
1.2.2.1.	Breton List	311	335	639	615	0	888	929
1.2.2.2.	Breton SE	309	321	629	610	888	0	949
1.2.2.3.	Breton ST	319	328	641	617	929	949	0

The full table is shown as Appendix 5. The % signs and the decimal points are omitted from the table entries for simplicity, both here and in the full table. This table contains lines corresponding to the classification, but the full table does not. The lexicostatistical method means computing a table like this one and using some unspecified systematic procedure to obtain a classification of the speech varieties.

Lexicostatistical percentages have also been used to calculate the dates at which the separations between different speech varieties occurred. This method, known as glottochronology, is not used in this work. Glottochronology depends on additional assumptions, and in our view is clearly less reliable than the use of lexicostatistics to make a classification.

One additional assumption that has been used almost universally in glottochronology is that all meanings in the Swadesh list are subject to the same replacement rate. This assumption is an oversimplification that is now known to be substantially in error, as shown in Dyen, James, and Cole (1967) and Kruskal, Dyen, and Black (1973). It accounts for many, perhaps most, of the anomalies that have been observed in the application of glottochronology. It can be replaced by a more realistic assumption, in which replacement rates are drawn from some probability distribution. It is even possible, for a wide variety of such distributions, to calculate an explicit formula for the relationship between time and lexicostatistical percentage. The methods for doing these things are widely known in the study of radioactive decay, and are based on well-known standard mathematics. (Appendix 7 draws slightly on these ideas.) Even if an improved assumption about replacement rates is used, however, glottochronology would still depend on further assumptions not needed in using lexicostatistics to make a classification.

A4. THE WORD LISTS AND THEIR SOURCES

The listing is in alphabetical order. The number of Swadesh meanings glossed in each list is shown in parentheses after the name of the list.

Afghan (200). P. B. Zudin, *Russko-Afganskij Slovar'*. Moscow, 1955.

Afrikaans (200). T. Kriel, *Die Nuwe Afrikaanse Skool-Wordenboek.* Kaapstad, 1945.

Albanian C (190). Piana degli Albanesi, Sicily; Eric Hamp.

Albanian K (200). Sophikon, Korinthia, Greece; Eric Hamp.

Albanian G (190). Geg dialect; G. Weigand, *Albanesisch-deutsches, deutsch-albanesisches Wörterbuch.* Leipzig, 1914.

Albanian T (198). Tosk dialect; Georges Schmidt.

Albanian Top (200). Ogrén/Përmét; Eric Hamp.

Armenian List (190). Adapazar dialect; V. Gerrard.

Armenian Mod (196). Eastern Modern Armenian; Ilya Abuladze in Knut Bergsland and Hans Vogt, "On the validity of glottochronology." *Current Anthropology* 3.2.115-153 (1962).

Baluchi (193). G. W. Gilbertson, *English-Balochi Colloquial Dictionary.* Hertford, 1925.

Bengali (198). Frank Southworth.

Brazilian (197). M. Reno, *Portuguese: A Handbook of Brazilian Conversation.* Chicago, 1943.

H. Limas and G. Barroso, *Pequenho dicionário brasileiro de lingua portuguesa.* Rio de Janeiro, 1949.

Breton List (199). F. Vallée, *Vocabulaire français-breton.* St.-Brieuc, 1919.

Breton SE (198). Vannes dialect; M. Piette.

Breton ST (198). Standard Breton; M. Piette.

Bulgarian (199). Sofia dialect; Kamen Ganchev.

Byelorussian (199). Eugene Botas.

Catalan (197). José Pujal y Serra, *Diccionairo Catalán-Castellano.* Barcelona, 1911.

Creole, see French Creole.

Czech (199). Tatyana Fedorow.

Czech E (199). Trnovec, Slovakia; Alfons Duffek.

Danish (200). Isidore Dyen.

Dutch List (199). Isidore Dyen.

English ST (200). Modern English.

Faroese (197). Jóhan Hendrik Poulsen, Halgir Winther Poulsen, and Waldemar Dalsgard via Wayne A. O'Neil.

Flemish (197). L'Abbé Olinger, *Nouveau Dictionnaire de poche français-flamand*. Malines, 1852.
French (200). Isidore Dyen.
French Creole C (196). Dominican French; Mervyn C. Alleyne.
French Creole D (200). Dominica, B. W. I.; Douglas Taylor.
Frisian (191). P. Sipma and Y. Poortinga, *Lyts Frysk Wirdboek*. Boalsert, 1944.
German ST (199). Standard German; Isidore Dyen.
Greek D (198). Demotiki; A. P. D. Mourelatos.
Greek K (198). Katharevousa; A. P. D. Mourelatos.
Greek MD (195). D. C. Swanson, *Vocabulary of Modern Spoken Greek*. Minneapolis, 1959.
Greek ML (199). Modern Standard Lesbian Greek; Demetrios Tsernoglou via E. W. Barber.
Greek Mod (200). Modern Greek; Renée Kahane.
Gujarati (194). Naik via George Cardona.
Gypsy Gk (183). Greek Gypsy; G. Drachman.
Hindi (200). Frank Southworth.
Icelandic ST (195). Standard Icelandic, Rejkjawik and rural dialects; Knut Bergsland and Hans Vogt, "On the validity of glottochronology." *Current Anthropology* 3.2.115-153 (1962).
Irish A (199). Miles Dillon.
Irish B (194). T. O. Lane, *Lane's English-Irish Dictionary*. Dublin, 1904.
Italian (199). Isidore Dyen.
Kashmiri (195). G. A. Grierson, *A Dictionary of the Kashmiri Language*. Calcutta, 1932.
Khaskura (187). G. W. P. Money, *Gurkhali Manual*. Bombay, 1942.
Ladin (198). Romanche; Ant. Velleman, *Dicziunari Scurzieu de la Lingua Ladina*. Samaden, 1929.
Lahnda (199). Rishi Gopal Ghatia.
Latvian (199). Riga; K. D. Hramov.
Lithuanian O (199). Vitalia Onopiak.
Lithuanian ST (200). Alfred Senn.
Lusatian L (192). Lower Lusatian; Fodor (1961) Table 2 (opp. p. 334).
Lusatian U (192). Upper Lusatian; Fodor (1961) Table 2 (opp. p. 335).
Macedonian (192). H. G. Hunt, *A Grammar of the Macedonian Literary Language*. Skopje, 1952.
Marathi (200). Frank Southworth.
Nepali List (198). R. L. Turner, *A Comparative and Etymological Dictionary of the Nepali Language*. London, 1931.

[Norwegian] Riksmal, see Riksmal.

Ossetic (184). V. I. Abaev, *Russko-Osetinskij Slovar'*. Moscow, 1950.

Panjabi ST (199). Frank Southworth.

Pennsylvania Dutch (191). E. R. Danner, *Pennsylvania Dutch Dictionary*. York, 1951.

Persian List (197). F. Kazemzadeh.

Polish (200). Alexander Schenker.

Portuguese ST (200). H. Michaelis, *A New Dictionary of the Portuguese and English Languages*. London, 1893.

Provençal (200). R. P. Xavier de Fourvières, *Lou Pichot tresor, dictionnaire provençal-français-provençal*. Avignon, 1902.

Riksmal (198). Knut Bergsland and Hans Vogt, "On the validity of glottochronology." *Current Anthropology* 3.2.115-153 (1962).

Rumanian List (200). Serban Andronescu, *Dictionar de Buzunar Englesz-Romîn*. Bucharest, 1961.

Russian (200). Alexander Schenker.

Sardinian C (200). Cagliari dialect; Frederick B. Agard.

Sardinian L (200). Logudorese dialect; Dietmar Vogel.

Sardinian N (198). Nuorese (Bitti) dialect; Frederick B. Agard.

Serbocroatian (200). Gordana Dimitrijević Lam.

Singhalese (200). B. Anuruddha Vajirarāma, Colombo, Ceylon.

Slovak (200). Tatyana Fedorow.

Slovenian (199). Ljubljana dialect; C. Grote.

Spanish (200). A. Cuyás, *Appleton's New English-Spanish and Spanish-English Dictionary*. New York, 1940.

Swedish List (199). K. Karre et al., *English-Swedish Dictionary*. Stockholm, 1935.

Swedish Up (200). Uppland dialect; Manne Eriksson.

Swedish VL (199). Vilhelmina, Southern Lapland; Rune Vasterlund.

Tadžik (196). D. Arzumznov and X. K. Karimov, *Russko-Tadžikskij Slovar'*. Moscow, 1957.

Takitaki (193). H. R. Wullschlägel, *Deutsch-Negerenglisches Wörterbuch*. Löbau, 1856.

Ukrainian (200). W. Luciw.

Vlach (183). Samarina; G. Drachman.

Wakhi (177). D. L. R. Lorimer, *The Wakhi Language*. London, 1958.

Walloon (198). J. Haust, *Dictionnaire Français-Liègeois*. Liège, 1948.

Waziri (184). John Gordon Lorimer, *Grammar and Vocabulary of Waziri Pashto*. Calcutta, 1902.

Welsh C (200). Carmarthen dialect; J. C. Stephens.

Welsh N (199). Bangor, North Wales; Hynel Bebb.

A5. TABLE OF LEXICOSTATISTICAL PERCENTAGES

There are 84 rows and columns on 16 pages. Parts 1,1 to 1,4 show the first 23 rows.

PART 1,1

		1.1.1.	1.1.2.	1.2.1.1.	1.2.1.2.	1.2.2.1.	1.2.2.2.	1.2.2.3.	2.1.1.1.	2.1.1.2.	2.1.2.1.	2.1.2.2.	2.1.2.3.1.	2.1.2.3.2.	2.1.2.3.3.	2.1.2.4.1.	2.1.2.4.2.	2.1.2.5.	2.1.2.6.1.	2.1.2.6.2.	2.1.2.7.1.	2.1.2.7.2.1.	2.1.2.7.2.2.	2.1.2.8.
		Iri sh A	Iri sh B	Wel sh N	Wel sh C	Bre ton Lst	Bre ton SE	Bre ton ST	Rum ani Lst	Vla ch	Ita lia n	Lad in	Pro ven cal	Fre nch	Wal loo n	Fr. Cre C	Fr. Cre D	Sar din N	Sar din L	Sar din C	Spa nis h	Por tug ST	Bra zil ian	Cat ala n
1.1.1.	Irish A	0	826	344	342	311	309	319	149	145	179	165	168	163	168	123	124	155	168	154	168	163	166	155
1.1.2.	Irish B	826	0	355	360	335	321	328	163	160	200	179	193	188	193	147	150	175	188	180	195	183	193	176
1.2.1.1.	Welsh N	344	355	0	939	639	629	641	188	189	207	199	195	190	195	176	174	194	207	194	187	196	200	182
1.2.1.2.	Welsh C	342	360	939	0	615	610	617	193	193	211	203	199	194	199	175	173	198	211	197	190	200	203	187
1.2.2.1.	Breton List	311	335	639	615	0	888	929	212	202	236	218	224	214	219	201	199	223	236	222	219	219	223	207
1.2.2.2.	Breton SE	309	321	629	610	888	0	949	212	209	226	212	214	204	209	191	188	212	226	211	209	214	218	202
1.2.2.3.	Breton ST	319	328	641	617	929	949	0	214	210	232	219	221	210	215	197	195	219	232	218	215	221	224	208
2.1.1.1.	Rumanian List	149	163	188	193	212	212	214	0	723	660	643	622	579	584	513	513	577	602	598	594	629	608	577
2.1.1.2.	Vlach	145	160	189	193	202	209	210	723	0	592	562	562	511	525	472	483	528	539	542	531	547	537	540
2.1.2.1.	Italian	179	200	207	211	236	226	232	660	592	0	832	818	803	774	697	689	728	797	731	788	773	785	764
2.1.2.2.	Ladin	165	179	199	203	218	212	219	643	562	832	0	760	740	731	653	660	655	687	662	716	731	722	696
2.1.2.3.1.	Provencal	168	193	195	199	224	214	221	622	562	818	760	0	899	839	799	792	656	701	675	731	721	733	737
2.1.2.3.2.	French	163	188	190	194	214	204	210	579	511	803	740	899	0	894	847	825	648	702	667	734	709	730	714
2.1.2.3.3.	Walloon	168	193	195	199	219	209	215	584	525	774	731	839	894	0	781	772	626	673	638	700	685	701	699
2.1.2.4.1.	Fr. Creole C	123	147	176	175	201	191	197	513	472	697	653	799	847	781	0	974	577	610	602	643	628	637	627
2.1.2.4.2.	Fr. Creole D	124	150	174	173	199	188	195	513	483	689	660	792	825	772	974	0	563	596	582	634	624	639	628
2.1.2.5.	Sardinian N	155	175	194	198	223	212	219	577	528	728	655	656	648	626	577	563	0	796	786	633	640	644	637
2.1.2.6.1.	Sardinian L	168	188	207	211	236	226	232	602	539	797	687	701	702	673	610	596	796	0	832	667	646	662	651
2.1.2.6.2.	Sardinian C	154	180	194	197	222	211	218	598	542	731	662	675	667	638	602	582	786	832	0	657	646	646	626
2.1.2.7.1.	Spanish	168	195	187	190	219	209	215	594	531	788	716	731	734	700	643	634	633	667	657	0	874	862	730
2.1.2.7.2.1.	Portuguese ST	163	183	196	200	219	214	221	629	547	773	731	721	709	685	628	624	640	646	646	874	0	969	708
2.1.2.7.2.2.	Brazilian	166	193	200	203	223	218	224	608	537	785	722	733	730	701	637	639	644	662	646	862	969	0	706
2.1.2.8.	Catalan	155	176	182	187	207	202	208	577	540	764	696	737	714	699	627	628	637	651	626	730	708	706	0
		Iri sh A	Iri sh B	Wel sh N	Wel sh C	Bre ton Lst	Bre ton SE	Bre ton ST	Rum ani Lst	Vla ch	Ita lia n	Lad in	Pro ven cal	Fre nch	Wal loo n	Fr. Cre C	Fr. Cre D	Sar din N	Sar din L	Sar din C	Spa nis h	Por tug ST	Bra zil ian	Cat ala n

PART 1,2

		2.2.1.1.1.	2.2.1.1.2.	2.2.1.1.3.1.	2.2.1.1.3.2.	2.2.1.1.3.3.	2.2.1.1.4.	2.2.1.2.1.1.1.	2.2.1.2.1.1.2.	2.2.1.2.1.1.3.	2.2.1.2.1.2.	2.2.1.2.1.3.	2.2.1.2.2.1.	2.2.1.2.2.2.	2.2.2.1.	2.2.2.2.	2.3.1.1.1.	2.3.1.1.2.	2.3.1.2.
		Ger man ST	Pen Dut ch	Dut ch Lst	Afr ika ans	Fle mis h	Fri sia n	Swe dis Up	Swe dis VL	Swe dis Lst	Dan ish	Rik sma l	Ice lan ST	Far oes e	Eng lis ST	Tak ita ki	Lit hua O	Lit hua ST	Lat via n
1.1.1.	Irish A	179	164	170	169	176	165	189	190	191	189	170	194	180	179	156	191	189	170
1.1.2.	Irish B	194	171	180	179	181	175	184	184	186	183	164	184	170	183	160	198	196	176
1.2.1.1.	Welsh N	180	156	160	161	168	167	165	166	181	175	151	180	173	159	160	189	193	158
1.2.1.2.	Welsh C	185	160	164	165	172	171	169	170	186	179	150	184	177	163	164	188	186	156
1.2.2.1.	Breton List	206	187	186	191	188	188	171	177	193	191	172	185	183	169	164	182	191	155
1.2.2.2.	Breton SE	205	187	185	190	188	194	174	180	196	195	176	189	188	179	176	187	190	160
1.2.2.3.	Breton ST	206	188	186	191	188	194	180	187	202	196	177	196	194	179	176	188	192	161
2.1.1.1.	Rumanian List	249	234	254	249	232	229	222	218	239	237	214	223	216	227	212	199	203	179
2.1.1.2.	Vlach	247	229	249	247	244	240	236	232	236	236	222	229	218	240	211	219	218	202
2.1.2.1.	Italian	265	250	260	259	251	245	254	250	259	263	246	245	242	247	215	234	242	218
2.1.2.2.	Ladin	250	241	246	246	234	231	240	236	251	249	227	230	224	239	212	219	218	209
2.1.2.3.1.	Provencal	249	233	244	247	251	238	258	259	254	246	235	244	247	231	198	227	221	207
2.1.2.3.2.	French	244	233	244	242	246	233	242	244	244	241	230	228	236	236	203	227	221	207
2.1.2.3.3.	Walloon	249	238	244	242	251	238	247	249	249	246	235	233	241	241	208	222	216	207
2.1.2.4.1.	Fr. Creole C	205	198	209	206	209	194	223	221	215	208	205	203	222	198	184	184	178	158
2.1.2.4.2.	Fr. Creole D	208	196	207	209	218	201	222	219	214	206	208	201	215	201	186	192	186	166
2.1.2.5.	Sardinian N	241	230	241	241	234	231	224	221	231	234	216	215	223	232	212	213	212	198
2.1.2.6.1.	Sardinian L	244	229	239	239	232	229	232	228	239	241	224	223	226	230	209	231	235	211
2.1.2.6.2.	Sardinian C	250	235	245	245	233	230	228	224	240	242	221	219	222	236	216	227	226	207
2.1.2.7.1.	Spanish	253	247	258	256	245	232	241	237	253	250	239	237	230	240	207	226	230	206
2.1.2.7.2.1.	Portuguese ST	247	242	253	251	240	232	241	237	258	250	239	237	235	240	212	221	215	196
2.1.2.7.2.2.	Brazilian	246	241	251	250	244	230	245	241	251	249	237	234	238	244	216	219	213	204
2.1.2.8.	Catalan	236	219	236	240	238	225	245	241	246	239	232	241	229	223	195	204	208	199
		Ger man ST	Pen Dut ch	Dut ch Lst	Afr ika ans	Fle mis h	Fri sia n	Swe dis Up	Swe dis VL	Swe dis Lst	Dan ish	Rik sma l	Ice lan ST	Far oes e	Eng lis ST	Tak ita ki	Lit hua O	Lit hua ST	Lat via n

PART 1,3

		2.3.2.1.	2.3.2.2.1.1.	2.3.2.2.1.2.	2.3.2.2.2.1.1.	2.3.2.2.2.1.2.	2.3.2.2.2.2.	2.3.2.2.3.1.	2.3.2.2.3.2.	2.3.2.2.4.	2.3.2.2.5.	2.3.2.2.6.1.	2.3.2.2.6.2.	2.3.2.2.6.3.	3.1.	3.2.	3.3.1.	3.3.2.1.1.1.	3.3.2.1.1.2.	3.3.2.1.2.1.1.	3.3.2.1.2.1.2.	3.3.2.1.2.2.	3.3.2.1.3.	3.3.2.2.1.	3.3.2.2.2.
		Slovenian	Lusati L	Lusati U	Czech	Slovak	Czech E	Ukrainian	Byelouss	Polish	Russian	Macedonia	Bulgarian	Serbocroa	Gypsy Gk	Singhales	Kashmiri	Marathi	Gujarati	Panjab ST	Lahnda	Hindi	Bengali	Nepali Lst	Khaskura
1.1.1.	Irish A	180	173	178	174	173	162	181	173	173	192	200	171	182	101	102	118	118	111	119	119	119	119	128	115
1.1.2.	Irish B	191	206	211	212	205	189	214	200	200	218	207	182	204	109	99	121	121	114	117	122	122	122	131	118
1.2.1.1.	Welsh N	162	185	185	200	194	185	188	184	178	182	187	162	179	97	87	129	107	101	115	114	124	119	115	122
1.2.1.2.	Welsh C	171	188	188	203	197	188	192	188	181	186	190	166	182	96	92	129	112	105	119	119	129	124	119	122
1.2.2.1.	Breton List	182	201	201	211	199	197	194	196	188	198	202	177	199	101	97	134	118	105	125	124	135	130	130	139
1.2.2.2.	Breton SE	181	199	199	209	198	195	193	194	188	196	207	181	198	107	102	138	122	110	130	130	140	135	135	139
1.2.2.3.	Breton ST	182	200	201	211	199	196	194	195	188	197	209	182	199	108	103	140	123	110	131	130	141	135	135	140
2.1.1.1.	Rumanian List	210	230	230	223	227	214	201	212	216	219	222	202	222	134	136	161	162	141	173	168	173	168	168	147
2.1.1.2.	Vlach	236	244	244	233	237	229	220	226	237	236	240	225	236	127	144	171	166	144	172	168	172	167	173	165
2.1.2.1.	Italian	240	250	250	247	251	236	226	237	236	239	250	231	245	133	152	173	167	152	184	183	182	173	178	168
2.1.2.2.	Ladin	227	251	251	240	249	234	223	234	233	236	254	234	238	133	146	169	179	158	180	180	189	179	179	159
2.1.2.3.1.	Provencal	213	222	222	221	224	214	214	210	214	217	217	209	218	133	146	161	160	145	177	176	175	172	172	151
2.1.2.3.2.	French	218	233	233	231	235	219	219	221	219	222	228	209	228	133	146	161	161	146	178	177	176	173	167	146
2.1.2.3.3.	Walloon	217	226	226	226	230	214	223	219	218	217	226	208	228	133	146	166	160	145	177	176	175	172	167	146
2.1.2.4.1.	Fr. Creole C	179	182	182	176	180	171	179	171	175	179	177	166	180	106	121	140	126	120	137	136	141	137	132	125
2.1.2.4.2.	Fr. Creole D	188	190	190	184	188	179	188	179	183	187	186	174	188	107	122	141	128	122	139	138	143	139	134	127
2.1.2.5.	Sardinian N	216	230	230	227	231	218	206	218	216	219	237	211	236	135	136	153	163	149	175	164	174	160	169	148
2.1.2.6.1.	Sardinian L	234	242	242	240	244	230	218	230	228	231	254	230	249	133	145	168	167	147	173	172	177	168	178	168
2.1.2.6.2.	Sardinian C	231	239	239	236	240	227	215	227	231	234	246	221	240	134	141	157	157	143	164	163	168	159	168	148
2.1.2.7.1.	Spanish	228	247	247	240	244	234	218	230	228	231	237	218	232	128	141	166	161	146	179	182	181	173	177	162
2.1.2.7.2.1.	Portuguese ST	219	243	243	236	240	230	219	226	224	227	238	219	234	128	146	171	166	151	184	183	187	173	177	157
2.1.2.7.2.2.	Brazilian	222	241	241	238	242	227	222	228	227	230	234	216	236	129	143	174	168	153	187	185	189	175	179	159
2.1.2.8.	Catalan	211	225	225	223	227	215	201	212	216	219	219	206	215	129	138	163	168	153	180	179	179	165	174	153
		Slovenian	Lusati L	Lusati U	Czech	Slovak	Czech E	Ukrainian	Byelouss	Polish	Russian	Macedonia	Bulgarian	Serbocroa	Gypsy Gk	Singhales	Kashmiri	Marathi	Gujarati	Panjab ST	Lahnda	Hindi	Bengali	Nepali Lst	Khaskura

PART 1,4

		4. 1. 1.	4. 1. 2.	4. 1. 3.	4. 1. 4.	4. 2.	5. 1.	5. 2.	6. 1.	6. 2. 1. 1.	6. 2. 1. 2.	6. 2. 2. 1. 1.	6. 2. 2. 1. 2.	6. 2. 2. 2.	6. 2. 2. 3.	7. 1. 1. 1.	7. 1. 1. 2.	7. 1. 2.	7. 2.	7. 3.
		Gre ek ML	Gre ek MD	Gre ek Mod	Gre ek D	Gre ek K	Arm eni Mod	Arm eni Lst	Oss eti c	Afg han	Waz iri	Per sia Lst	Tad zik	Bal uch i	Wak hi	Alb ani T	Alb ani Top	Alb ani G	Alb ani K	Alb ani C
1.1.1.	Irish A	133	151	142	144	159	120	112	111	93	91	104	120	100	82	95	99	104	98	109
1.1.2.	Irish B	131	150	141	142	159	122	109	103	105	93	112	129	109	90	98	107	106	101	111
1.2.1.1.	Welsh N	124	137	133	135	155	126	113	101	93	82	101	116	96	100	94	98	99	94	104
1.2.1.2.	Welsh C	128	141	138	140	160	131	118	106	92	87	105	121	101	105	94	98	98	94	104
1.2.2.1.	Breton List	134	147	144	146	166	126	112	102	98	92	105	121	100	105	105	108	110	104	115
1.2.2.2.	Breton SE	129	141	138	141	160	126	112	112	103	97	116	126	111	118	109	113	114	109	120
1.2.2.3.	Breton ST	130	142	139	141	166	126	112	118	104	98	116	127	111	118	109	114	115	110	121
2.1.1.1.	Rumanian List	147	150	157	154	168	136	118	138	94	98	136	137	132	149	109	113	115	113	125
2.1.1.2.	Vlach	178	177	183	180	191	149	129	139	103	107	149	157	138	150	119	124	124	124	129
2.1.2.1.	Italian	168	177	178	174	190	152	138	143	120	114	141	157	136	140	115	123	120	122	134
2.1.2.2.	Ladin	149	152	158	156	165	137	124	144	115	105	147	153	138	141	110	119	110	113	130
2.1.2.3.1.	Provencal	157	166	167	163	179	146	133	143	119	114	141	151	141	140	114	122	119	122	134
2.1.2.3.2.	French	147	155	157	153	168	146	133	143	119	114	141	151	141	139	114	122	120	122	134
2.1.2.3.3.	Walloon	147	155	157	153	168	146	133	148	119	114	141	156	135	145	114	122	119	122	134
2.1.2.4.1.	Fr. Creole C	117	125	122	124	138	120	112	99	83	76	105	111	110	122	83	88	88	88	98
2.1.2.4.2.	Fr. Creole D	119	127	124	126	141	122	114	101	85	77	106	112	112	123	85	89	89	89	99
2.1.2.5.	Sardinian N	144	147	153	151	165	132	119	133	99	99	126	137	126	135	111	120	117	119	131
2.1.2.6.1.	Sardinian L	157	166	172	165	184	135	122	131	108	103	130	145	130	139	120	129	126	128	141
2.1.2.6.2.	Sardinian C	153	156	157	161	174	136	124	132	98	98	125	131	132	129	110	114	122	108	125
2.1.2.7.1.	Spanish	157	166	167	163	173	145	132	144	113	108	140	145	141	134	108	117	114	111	128
2.1.2.7.2.1.	Portuguese ST	157	161	167	163	173	146	134	148	119	114	146	151	146	140	109	117	114	117	134
2.1.2.7.2.2.	Brazilian	154	162	163	160	170	147	134	145	120	115	142	147	142	140	115	124	121	118	135
2.1.2.8.	Catalan	149	153	154	150	166	147	134	144	120	115	142	147	142	140	110	113	115	118	130
		Gre ek ML	Gre ek MD	Gre ek Mod	Gre ek D	Gre ek K	Arm eni Mod	Arm eni Lst	Oss eti c	Afg han	Waz iri	Per sia Lst	Tad zik	Bal uch i	Wak hi	Alb ani T	Alb ani Top	Alb ani G	Alb ani K	Alb ani C

PART 2,1

		1.1.1.	1.1.2.	1.2.1.1.	1.2.1.2.	1.2.2.1.	1.2.2.2.	1.2.2.3.	2.1.1.1.	2.1.1.2.	2.1.2.1.	2.1.2.2.	2.1.2.3.1.	2.1.2.3.2.	2.1.2.3.3.	2.1.2.4.1.	2.1.2.4.2.	2.1.2.5.	2.1.2.6.1.	2.1.2.6.2.	2.1.2.7.1.	2.1.2.7.2.1.	2.1.2.7.2.2.	2.1.2.8.
		Iri sh A	Iri sh B	Wel sh N	Wel sh C	Bre ton Lst	Bre ton SE	Bre ton ST	Rum ani Lst	Vla ch	Ita lia n	Lad in	Pro ven cal	Fre nch	Wal loo n	Fr. Cre C	Fr. Cre D	Sar din N	Sar din L	Sar din C	Spa nis h	Por tug ST	Bra zil ian	Cat ala n
2.2.1.1.1.	German ST	179	194	180	185	206	205	206	249	247	265	250	249	244	249	205	208	241	244	250	253	247	246	236
2.2.1.1.2.	Penn. Dutch	164	171	156	160	187	187	188	234	229	250	241	233	233	238	198	196	230	229	235	247	242	241	219
2.2.1.1.3.1.	Dutch List	170	180	160	164	186	185	186	254	249	260	246	244	244	244	209	207	241	239	245	258	253	251	236
2.2.1.1.3.2.	Afrikaans	169	179	161	165	191	190	191	249	247	259	246	247	242	242	206	209	241	239	245	256	251	250	240
2.2.1.1.3.3.	Flemish	176	181	168	172	188	188	188	232	244	251	234	251	246	251	209	218	234	232	233	245	240	244	238
2.2.1.1.4.	Frisian	165	175	167	171	188	194	194	229	240	245	231	238	233	238	194	201	231	229	230	232	232	230	225
2.2.1.2.1.1.1.	Swedish Up	189	184	165	169	171	174	180	222	236	254	240	258	242	247	223	222	224	232	228	241	241	245	245
2.2.1.2.1.1.2.	Swedish VL	190	184	166	170	177	180	187	218	232	250	236	259	244	249	221	219	221	228	224	237	237	241	241
2.2.1.2.1.1.3.	Swedish List	191	186	181	186	193	196	202	239	236	259	251	254	244	249	215	214	231	239	240	253	258	251	246
2.2.1.2.1.2.	Danish	189	183	175	179	191	195	196	237	236	263	249	246	241	246	208	206	234	241	242	250	250	249	239
2.2.1.2.1.3.	Riksmal	170	164	151	150	172	176	177	214	222	246	227	235	230	235	205	208	216	224	221	239	239	237	232
2.2.1.2.2.1.	Icelandic ST	194	184	180	184	185	189	196	223	229	245	230	244	228	233	203	201	215	223	219	237	237	234	241
2.2.1.2.2.2.	Faroese	180	170	173	177	183	188	194	216	218	242	224	247	236	241	222	215	223	226	222	230	235	238	229
2.2.2.1.	English ST	179	183	159	163	169	179	179	227	240	247	239	231	236	241	198	201	232	230	236	240	240	244	223
2.2.2.2.	Takitaki	156	160	160	164	164	176	176	212	211	215	212	198	203	208	184	186	212	209	216	207	212	216	195
2.3.1.1.1.	Lithuanian O	191	198	189	188	182	187	188	199	219	234	219	227	227	222	184	192	213	231	227	226	221	219	204
2.3.1.1.2.	Lithuanian ST	189	196	193	186	191	190	192	203	218	242	218	221	221	216	178	186	212	235	226	230	215	213	208
2.3.1.2.	Latvian	170	176	158	156	155	160	161	179	202	218	209	207	207	207	158	166	198	211	207	206	196	204	199
		Iri sh A	Iri sh B	Wel sh N	Wel sh C	Bre ton Lst	Bre ton SE	Bre ton ST	Rum ani Lst	Vla ch	Ita lia n	Lad in	Pro ven cal	Fre nch	Wal loo n	Fr. Cre C	Fr. Cre D	Sar din N	Sar din L	Sar din C	Spa nis h	Por tug ST	Bra zil ian	Cat ala n

PART 2,2

		2. 2. 1. 1. 1.	2. 2. 1. 1. 2.	2. 2. 1. 1. 3. 1.	2. 2. 1. 1. 3. 2.	2. 2. 1. 1. 3. 3.	2. 2. 1. 1. 4.	2. 2. 1. 2. 1. 1. 1.	2. 2. 1. 2. 1. 1. 2.	2. 2. 1. 2. 1. 1. 3.	2. 2. 1. 2. 1. 2.	2. 2. 1. 2. 1. 3.	2. 2. 1. 2. 2. 1.	2. 2. 1. 2. 2. 2.	2. 2. 2. 1.	2. 2. 2. 2.	2. 3. 1. 1. 1.	2. 3. 1. 1. 2.	2. 3. 1. 2.
		Ger man ST	Pen Dut ch	Dut ch Lst	Afr ika ans	Fle mis h	Fri sia n	Swe dis Up	Swe dis VL	Swe dis Lst	Dan ish	Rik sma l	Ice lan ST	Far oes e	Eng lis ST	Tak ita ki	Lit hua O	Lit hua ST	Lat via n
2.2.1.1.1.	German ST	0	858	838	844	837	751	631	624	695	707	633	591	593	578	573	221	224	200
2.2.1.1.2.	Penn. Dutch	858	0	779	800	777	720	571	543	601	624	599	565	576	553	568	190	201	181
2.2.1.1.3.1.	Dutch List	838	779	0	965	954	797	648	621	692	663	650	582	582	608	589	200	214	195
2.2.1.1.3.2.	Afrikaans	844	800	965	0	970	824	640	618	693	670	646	585	587	605	601	204	218	199
2.2.1.1.3.3.	Flemish	837	777	954	970	0	844	629	607	680	665	646	583	591	589	589	206	215	196
2.2.1.1.4.	Frisian	751	720	797	824	844	0	571	564	638	614	606	554	551	561	557	197	202	193
2.2.1.2.1.1.1.	Swedish Up	631	571	648	640	629	571	0	925	910	830	838	800	811	591	492	213	202	193
2.2.1.2.1.1.2.	Swedish VL	624	543	621	618	607	564	925	0	904	809	817	784	820	566	453	219	208	194
2.2.1.2.1.1.3.	Swedish List	695	601	692	693	680	638	910	904	0	874	842	789	800	589	497	230	218	209
2.2.1.2.1.2.	Danish	707	624	663	670	665	614	830	809	874	0	854	779	786	593	518	228	222	203
2.2.1.2.1.3.	Riksmal	633	599	650	646	646	606	838	817	842	854	0	809	821	548	482	205	204	185
2.2.1.2.2.1.	Icelandic ST	591	565	582	585	583	554	800	784	789	779	809	0	922	546	463	208	202	188
2.2.1.2.2.2.	Faroese	593	576	582	587	591	551	811	820	800	786	821	922	0	536	463	196	190	175
2.2.2.1.	English ST	578	553	608	605	589	561	591	566	589	593	548	546	536	0	658	212	216	197
2.2.2.2.	Takitaki	573	568	589	601	589	557	492	453	497	518	482	463	463	658	0	164	168	143
2.3.1.1.1.	Lithuanian O	221	190	200	204	206	197	213	219	230	228	205	208	196	212	164	0	899	561
2.3.1.1.2.	Lithuanian ST	224	201	214	218	215	202	202	208	218	222	204	202	190	216	168	899	0	613
2.3.1.2.	Latvian	200	181	195	199	196	193	193	194	209	203	185	188	175	197	143	561	613	0
		Ger man ST	Pen Dut ch	Dut ch Lst	Afr ika ans	Fle mis h	Fri sia n	Swe dis Up	Swe dis VL	Swe dis Lst	Dan ish	Rik sma l	Ice lan ST	Far oes e	Eng lis ST	Tak ita ki	Lit hua O	Lit hua ST	Lat via n

PART 2,3

		2.3.2.1.	2.3.2.2.1.1.	2.3.2.2.1.2.	2.3.2.2.2.1.1.	2.3.2.2.2.1.2.	2.3.2.2.2.2.	2.3.2.2.3.1.	2.3.2.2.3.2.	2.3.2.2.4.	2.3.2.2.5.	2.3.2.2.6.1.	2.3.2.2.6.2.	2.3.2.2.6.3.	3.1.	3.2.	3.3.1.	3.3.2.1.1.1.	3.3.2.1.1.2.	3.3.2.1.2.1.1.	3.3.2.1.2.1.2.	3.3.2.1.2.2.	3.3.2.1.3.	3.3.2.2.1.	3.3.2.2.2.
		Slovenian	Lusati L	Lusati U	Czech	Slovak	Czech E	Ukrainian	Byel
oruss	Polish	Russian	Macedonia	Bulgarian	Serbocroa	Gypsy Gk	Singhales	Kashmiri	Marathi	Gujarati	Panjab ST	Lahnda	Hindi	Bengali	Nepali Lst	Khaskura
2.2.1.1.1.	German ST	267	238	238	259	258	253	241	247	246	245	255	231	236	111	137	153	151	141	153	147	147	143	163	137
2.2.1.1.2.	Penn. Dutch	230	227	227	238	231	232	219	220	225	223	240	220	220	116	136	148	141	141	160	153	153	144	160	135
2.2.1.1.3.1.	Dutch List	246	223	223	244	247	232	215	237	231	224	229	221	221	106	137	152	152	136	154	143	143	144	158	131
2.2.1.1.3.2.	Afrikaans	250	233	233	247	251	237	219	241	240	234	239	221	231	100	131	146	136	125	153	142	142	138	147	130
2.2.1.1.3.3.	Flemish	253	225	225	245	238	234	222	228	232	226	247	228	223	107	138	153	147	137	155	143	143	139	160	132
2.2.1.1.4.	Frisian	230	210	210	232	231	222	209	226	219	218	235	215	215	99	121	141	136	130	144	132	132	128	154	135
2.2.1.2.1.1.1.	Swedish Up	246	229	229	233	242	227	236	237	236	245	255	235	236	106	126	158	140	145	163	157	157	142	162	147
2.2.1.2.1.1.2.	Swedish VL	242	214	214	234	244	223	227	238	227	236	246	226	227	106	127	148	141	141	144	147	142	138	162	141
2.2.1.2.1.1.3.	Swedish List	253	230	230	250	259	233	242	254	237	246	257	236	237	100	122	159	141	141	159	152	152	143	163	147
2.2.1.2.1.2.	Danish	267	239	239	254	268	247	241	258	251	260	271	240	251	106	126	163	145	140	163	157	157	147	168	152
2.2.1.2.1.3.	Riksmal	238	214	214	236	245	229	228	240	238	242	247	227	228	107	122	153	141	147	149	148	148	138	164	148
2.2.1.2.2.1.	Icelandic ST	237	217	217	234	243	238	232	238	242	246	255	225	232	102	130	157	144	133	147	145	145	141	167	145
2.2.1.2.2.2.	Faroese	219	199	199	221	225	220	229	220	219	228	243	212	219	102	128	144	127	126	140	138	138	134	155	138
2.2.2.1.	English ST	249	226	226	241	250	219	223	235	239	242	253	228	234	106	131	161	145	135	157	146	146	142	157	141
2.2.2.2.	Takitaki	195	185	185	196	195	191	199	189	194	188	203	180	190	85	104	118	114	108	121	109	115	110	121	107
2.3.1.1.1.	Lithuanian O	326	376	382	354	370	344	375	361	351	371	386	335	345	157	154	209	177	184	171	173	199	199	195	187
2.3.1.1.2.	Lithuanian ST	338	394	404	376	395	368	371	373	361	378	390	342	357	156	159	207	181	178	174	168	188	188	194	192
2.3.1.2.	Latvian	323	349	354	333	357	323	357	369	332	359	356	306	337	124	118	185	157	152	154	149	152	162	168	160
		Slovenian	Lusati L	Lusati U	Czech	Slovak	Czech E	Ukrainian	Byelouss	Polish	Russian	Macedonia	Bulgarian	Serbocroa	Gypsy Gk	Singhales	Kashmiri	Marathi	Gujarati	Panjab ST	Lahnda	Hindi	Bengali	Nepali Lst	Khaskura

PART 2,4

		4.1.1.	4.1.2.	4.1.3.	4.1.4.	4.2.	5.1.	5.2.	6.1.	6.2.1.1.	6.2.1.2.	6.2.2.1.1.	6.2.2.1.2.	6.2.2.2.	6.2.2.3.	7.1.1.1.	7.1.1.2.	7.1.2.	7.2.	7.3.
		Greek ML	Greek MD	Greek Mod	Greek D	Greek K	Armeni Mod	Armeni Lst	Osseti c	Afghan	Waziri	Persia Lst	Tadzik	Baluchi	Wakhi	Albani T	Albani Top	Albani G	Albani K	Albani C
2.2.1.1.1.	German ST	173	188	188	179	210	146	128	149	104	109	140	147	142	134	126	130	131	129	130
2.2.1.1.2.	Penn. Dutch	163	177	179	169	202	146	134	145	109	114	135	142	142	127	109	114	119	114	113
2.2.1.1.3.1.	Dutch List	173	194	188	184	215	146	139	149	104	103	146	147	142	140	111	109	116	113	114
2.2.1.1.3.2.	Afrikaans	162	177	172	173	204	140	138	154	104	103	145	146	135	133	110	109	116	113	114
2.2.1.1.3.3.	Flemish	163	190	179	175	207	141	139	150	105	104	147	153	132	129	116	115	122	120	121
2.2.1.1.4.	Frisian	159	174	175	166	198	146	133	124	97	101	114	131	115	114	120	118	125	124	125
2.2.1.2.1.1.1.	Swedish Up	168	188	183	168	205	156	144	148	93	98	135	146	130	133	104	103	114	108	114
2.2.1.2.1.1.2.	Swedish VL	168	177	178	174	200	152	144	148	93	97	135	146	131	134	120	119	124	118	130
2.2.1.2.1.1.3.	Swedish List	168	184	184	174	206	157	149	148	94	97	135	147	130	133	120	119	125	124	130
2.2.1.2.1.2.	Danish	168	182	183	179	200	151	144	142	98	103	140	151	141	127	121	125	131	130	130
2.2.1.2.1.3.	Riksmal	164	179	179	170	192	136	129	132	94	98	126	137	126	129	111	110	122	109	120
2.2.1.2.2.1.	Icelandic ST	182	198	198	194	216	160	148	140	101	106	138	151	145	132	108	107	118	106	117
2.2.1.2.2.2.	Faroese	180	189	190	192	207	163	157	139	95	100	132	143	138	130	106	105	116	105	115
2.2.2.1.	English ST	147	166	162	158	194	130	133	142	93	98	140	147	126	123	113	117	129	122	118
2.2.2.2.	Takitaki	115	134	130	127	153	117	114	108	74	77	101	108	113	114	86	90	95	96	90
2.3.1.1.1.	Lithuanian O	154	167	162	160	191	152	150	132	115	120	161	161	136	110	137	141	142	130	137
2.3.1.1.2.	Lithuanian ST	158	182	172	169	205	152	154	133	120	114	161	155	130	109	141	144	147	133	135
2.3.1.2.	Latvian	149	162	152	149	180	131	138	128	103	103	141	141	109	121	124	133	135	122	129
		Greek ML	Greek MD	Greek Mod	Greek D	Greek K	Armeni Mod	Armeni Lst	Osseti c	Afghan	Waziri	Persia Lst	Tadzik	Baluchi	Wakhi	Albani T	Albani Top	Albani G	Albani K	Albani C

PART 3,1

		1.1.1.	1.1.2.	1.2.1.1.	1.2.1.2.	1.2.2.1.	1.2.2.2.	1.2.2.3.	2.1.1.1.	2.1.1.2.	2.1.2.1.	2.1.2.2.	2.1.2.3.1.	2.1.2.3.2.	2.1.2.3.3.	2.1.2.4.1.	2.1.2.4.2.	2.1.2.5.	2.1.2.6.1.	2.1.2.6.2.	2.1.2.7.1.	2.1.2.7.2.1.	2.1.2.7.2.2.	2.1.2.8.
		Iri sh A	Iri sh B	Wel sh N	Wel sh C	Bre ton Lst	Bre ton SE	Bre ton ST	Rum ani Lst	Vla ch	Ita lia n	Lad in	Pro ven cal	Fre nch	Wal loo n	Fr. Cre C	Fr. Cre D	Sar din N	Sar din L	Sar din C	Spa nis h	Por tug ST	Bra zil ian	Cat ala n
2.3.2.1.	Slovenian	180	191	162	171	182	181	182	210	236	240	227	213	218	217	179	188	216	234	231	228	219	222	211
2.3.2.2.1.1.	Lusatian L	173	206	185	188	201	199	200	230	244	250	251	222	233	226	182	190	230	242	239	247	243	241	225
2.3.2.2.1.2.	Lusatian U	178	211	185	188	201	199	201	230	244	250	251	222	233	226	182	190	230	242	239	247	243	241	225
2.3.2.2.2.1.1.	Czech	174	212	200	203	211	209	211	223	233	247	240	221	231	226	176	184	227	240	236	240	236	238	223
2.3.2.2.2.1.2.	Slovak	173	205	194	197	199	198	199	227	237	251	249	224	235	230	180	188	231	244	240	244	240	242	227
2.3.2.2.2.2.	Czech E	162	189	185	188	197	195	196	214	229	236	234	214	219	214	171	179	218	230	227	234	230	227	215
2.3.2.2.3.1.	Ukrainian	181	214	188	192	194	193	194	201	220	226	223	214	219	223	179	188	206	218	215	218	219	222	201
2.3.2.2.3.2.	Byelorussian	173	200	184	188	196	194	195	212	226	237	234	210	221	219	171	179	218	230	227	230	226	228	212
2.3.2.2.4.	Polish	173	200	178	181	188	188	188	216	237	236	233	214	219	218	175	183	216	228	231	228	224	227	216
2.3.2.2.5.	Russian	192	218	182	186	198	196	197	219	236	239	236	217	222	217	179	187	219	231	234	231	227	230	219
2.3.2.2.6.1.	Macedonian	200	207	187	190	202	207	209	222	240	250	254	217	228	226	177	186	237	254	246	237	238	234	219
2.3.2.2.6.2.	Bulgarian	171	182	162	166	177	181	182	202	225	231	234	209	209	208	166	174	211	230	221	218	219	216	206
2.3.2.2.6.3.	Serbocroatian	182	204	179	182	199	198	199	222	236	245	238	218	228	228	180	188	236	249	240	232	234	236	215
3.1.	Gypsy Gk	101	109	97	96	101	107	108	134	127	133	133	133	133	133	106	107	135	133	134	128	128	129	129
3.2.	Singhalese	102	99	87	92	97	102	103	136	144	152	146	146	146	146	121	122	136	145	141	141	146	143	138
3.3.1.	Kashmiri	118	121	129	129	134	138	140	161	171	173	169	161	161	166	140	141	153	168	157	166	171	174	163
3.3.2.1.1.1.	Marathi	118	121	107	112	118	122	123	162	166	167	179	160	161	160	126	128	163	167	157	161	166	168	168
3.3.2.1.1.2.	Gujarati	111	114	101	105	105	110	110	141	144	152	158	145	146	145	120	122	149	147	143	146	151	153	153
3.3.2.1.2.1.1.	Panjabi ST	119	117	115	119	125	130	131	173	172	184	180	177	178	177	137	139	175	173	164	179	184	187	180
3.3.2.1.2.1.2.	Lahnda	119	122	114	119	124	130	130	168	168	183	180	176	177	176	136	138	164	172	163	182	183	185	179
3.3.2.1.2.2.	Hindi	119	122	124	129	135	140	141	173	172	182	189	175	176	175	141	143	174	177	168	181	187	189	179
3.3.2.1.3.	Bengali	119	122	119	124	130	135	135	168	167	173	179	172	173	172	137	139	160	168	159	173	173	175	165
3.3.2.2.1.	Nepali List	128	131	115	119	130	135	135	168	173	178	179	172	167	167	132	134	169	178	168	177	177	179	174
3.3.2.2.2.	Khaskura	115	118	122	122	139	139	140	147	165	168	159	151	146	146	125	127	148	168	148	162	157	159	153
		Iri sh A	Iri sh B	Wel sh N	Wel sh C	Bre ton Lst	Bre ton SE	Bre ton ST	Rum ani Lst	Vla ch	Ita lia n	Lad in	Pro ven cal	Fre nch	Wal loo n	Fr. Cre C	Fr. Cre D	Sar din N	Sar din L	Sar din C	Spa nis h	Por tug ST	Bra zil ian	Cat ala n

PART 3,2

		2.2.1.1.1.	2.2.1.1.2.	2.2.1.1.3.1.	2.2.1.1.3.2.	2.2.1.1.3.3.	2.2.1.1.4.	2.2.1.2.1.1.1.	2.2.1.2.1.1.2.	2.2.1.2.1.1.3.	2.2.1.2.1.2.	2.2.1.2.1.3.	2.2.1.2.2.1.	2.2.1.2.2.2.	2.2.2.1.	2.2.2.2.	2.3.1.1.1.	2.3.1.1.2.	2.3.1.2.
		Ger man ST	Pen Dut ch	Dut ch Lst	Afr ika ans	Fle mis h	Fri sia n	Swe dis Up	Swe dis VL	Swe dis Lst	Dan ish	Rik sma l	Ice lan ST	Far oes e	Eng lis ST	Tak ita ki	Lit hua O	Lit hua ST	Lat via n
2.3.2.1.	Slovenian	267	230	246	250	253	230	246	242	253	267	238	237	219	249	195	326	338	323
2.3.2.2.1.1.	Lusatian L	238	227	223	233	225	210	229	214	230	239	214	217	199	226	185	376	394	349
2.3.2.2.1.2.	Lusatian U	238	227	223	233	225	210	229	214	230	239	214	217	199	226	185	382	404	354
2.3.2.2.2.1.1.	Czech	259	238	244	247	245	232	233	234	250	254	236	234	221	241	196	354	376	333
2.3.2.2.2.1.2.	Slovak	258	231	247	251	238	231	242	244	259	268	245	243	225	250	195	370	395	357
2.3.2.2.2.2.	Czech E	253	232	232	237	234	222	227	223	233	247	229	238	220	219	191	344	368	323
2.3.2.2.3.1.	Ukrainian	241	219	215	219	222	209	236	227	242	241	228	232	229	223	199	375	371	357
2.3.2.2.3.2.	Byelorussian	247	220	237	241	228	226	237	238	254	258	240	238	220	235	189	361	373	369
2.3.2.2.4.	Polish	246	225	231	240	232	219	236	227	237	251	238	242	219	239	194	351	361	332
2.3.2.2.5.	Russian	245	223	224	234	226	218	245	236	246	260	242	246	228	242	188	371	378	359
2.3.2.2.6.1.	Macedonian	255	240	229	239	247	235	255	246	257	271	247	255	243	253	203	386	390	356
2.3.2.2.6.2.	Bulgarian	231	220	221	221	228	215	235	226	236	240	227	225	212	228	180	335	342	306
2.3.2.2.6.3.	Serbocroatian	236	220	221	231	223	215	236	227	237	251	228	232	219	234	190	345	357	337
3.1.	Gypsy Gk	111	116	106	100	107	99	106	106	100	106	107	102	102	106	85	157	156	124
3.2.	Singhalese	137	136	137	131	138	121	126	127	122	126	122	130	128	131	104	154	159	118
3.3.1.	Kashmiri	153	148	152	146	153	141	158	148	159	163	153	157	144	161	118	209	207	185
3.3.2.1.1.1.	Marathi	151	141	152	136	147	136	140	141	141	145	141	144	127	145	114	177	181	157
3.3.2.1.1.2.	Gujarati	141	141	136	125	137	130	145	141	141	140	147	133	126	135	108	184	178	152
3.3.2.1.2.1.1.	Panjabi ST	153	160	154	153	155	144	163	144	159	163	149	147	140	157	121	171	174	154
3.3.2.1.2.1.2.	Lahnda	147	153	143	142	143	132	157	147	152	157	148	145	138	146	109	173	168	149
3.3.2.1.2.2.	Hindi	147	153	143	142	143	132	157	142	152	157	148	145	138	146	115	199	188	152
3.3.2.1.3.	Bengali	143	144	144	138	139	128	142	138	143	147	138	141	134	142	110	199	188	162
3.3.2.2.1.	Nepali List	163	160	158	147	160	154	162	162	163	168	164	167	155	157	121	195	194	168
3.3.2.2.2.	Khaskura	137	135	131	130	132	135	147	141	147	152	148	145	138	141	107	187	192	160
		Ger man ST	Pen Dut ch	Dut ch Lst	Afr ika ans	Fle mis h	Fri sia n	Swe dis Up	Swe dis VL	Swe dis Lst	Dan ish	Rik sma l	Ice lan ST	Far oes e	Eng lis ST	Tak ita ki	Lit hua O	Lit hua ST	Lat via n

PART 3,3

		Slo ven ian	Lus ati L	Lus ati U	Cze ch	Slo vak	Cze ch E	Ukr ain ian	Bye lor uss	Pol ish	Rus sia n	Mac edo nia	Bul gar ian	Ser boc roa	Gyp sy Gk	Sin gha les	Kas hmi ri	Mar ath i	Guj ara ti	Pan jab ST	Lah nda	Hin di	Ben gal i	Nep ali Lst	Kha sku ra
		2.3.2.1.	2.3.2.2.1.1.	2.3.2.2.1.2.	2.3.2.2.2.1.1.	2.3.2.2.2.1.2.	2.3.2.2.2.2.	2.3.2.2.3.1.	2.3.2.2.3.2.	2.3.2.2.4.	2.3.2.2.5.	2.3.2.2.6.1.	2.3.2.2.6.2.	2.3.2.2.6.3.	3.1.	3.2.	3.3.1.	3.3.2.1.1.1.	3.3.2.1.1.2.	3.3.2.1.2.1.1.	3.3.2.1.2.1.2.	3.3.2.1.2.2.	3.3.2.1.3.	3.3.2.2.1.	3.3.2.2.2.
2.3.2.1.	Slovenian	0	679	684	663	694	685	645	610	633	614	691	615	684	147	152	190	183	178	175	186	200	173	199	196
2.3.2.2.1.1.	Lusatian L	679	0	958	814	800	788	770	720	768	728	795	688	754	163	148	200	185	186	199	199	219	196	202	199
2.3.2.2.1.2.	Lusatian U	684	958	0	830	816	810	780	735	768	743	795	698	749	163	148	206	185	186	199	199	219	197	203	200
2.3.2.2.2.1.1.	Czech	663	814	830	0	914	883	763	735	766	745	749	689	719	153	144	194	179	176	183	181	203	187	203	194
2.3.2.2.2.1.2.	Slovak	694	800	816	914	0	874	813	779	778	741	762	685	732	153	148	198	184	180	181	181	201	186	197	188
2.3.2.2.2.2.	Czech E	685	788	810	883	874	0	753	714	737	706	722	672	694	141	138	182	173	169	172	171	192	175	192	181
2.3.2.2.3.1.	Ukrainian	645	770	780	763	813	753	0	839	802	779	742	660	707	152	137	186	168	173	175	180	195	184	191	181
2.3.2.2.3.2.	Byelorussian	610	720	735	735	779	714	839	0	751	732	686	646	673	141	138	188	169	180	172	176	192	175	192	182
2.3.2.2.4.	Polish	633	768	768	766	778	737	802	751	0	734	697	631	680	152	148	196	173	179	181	187	201	185	201	193
2.3.2.2.5.	Russian	614	728	743	745	741	706	779	732	734	0	720	635	675	151	147	191	183	173	180	180	200	189	200	191
2.3.2.2.6.1.	Macedonian	691	795	795	749	762	722	742	686	697	720	0	835	825	157	153	220	206	189	182	187	207	190	217	205
2.3.2.2.6.2.	Bulgarian	615	688	698	689	685	672	660	646	631	635	835	0	709	152	148	203	189	183	175	179	199	173	209	197
2.3.2.2.6.3.	Serbocroatian	684	754	749	719	732	694	707	673	680	675	825	709	0	145	152	191	178	173	175	179	195	173	189	180
3.1.	Gypsy Gk	147	163	163	153	153	141	152	141	152	151	157	152	145	0	188	268	268	267	278	280	305	273	339	292
3.2.	Singhalese	152	148	148	144	148	138	137	138	148	147	153	148	152	188	0	242	255	253	237	236	259	279	296	283
3.3.1.	Kashmiri	190	200	206	194	198	182	186	188	196	191	220	203	191	268	242	0	364	397	394	408	424	410	495	427
3.3.2.1.1.1.	Marathi	183	185	185	179	184	173	168	169	173	183	206	189	178	268	255	364	0	613	492	469	564	550	552	431
3.3.2.1.1.2.	Gujarati	178	186	186	176	180	169	173	180	179	173	189	183	173	267	253	397	613	0	543	561	646	535	587	455
3.3.2.1.2.1.1.	Panjabi ST	175	199	199	183	181	172	175	172	181	180	182	175	175	278	237	394	492	543	0	770	745	551	577	466
3.3.2.1.2.1.2.	Lahnda	186	199	199	181	181	171	180	176	187	180	187	179	179	280	236	408	469	561	770	0	714	521	562	453
3.3.2.1.2.2.	Hindi	200	219	219	203	201	192	195	192	201	200	207	199	195	305	259	424	564	646	745	714	0	641	642	534
3.3.2.1.3.	Bengali	173	196	197	187	186	175	184	175	185	189	190	173	173	273	279	410	550	535	551	521	641	0	603	511
3.3.2.2.1.	Nepali List	199	202	203	203	197	192	191	192	201	200	217	209	189	339	296	495	552	587	577	562	642	603	0	852
3.3.2.2.2.	Khaskura	196	199	200	194	188	181	181	182	193	191	205	197	180	292	283	427	431	455	466	453	534	511	852	0
		Slo ven ian	Lus ati L	Lus ati U	Cze ch	Slo vak	Cze ch E	Ukr ain ian	Bye lor uss	Pol ish	Rus sia n	Mac edo nia	Bul gar ian	Ser boc roa	Gyp sy Gk	Sin gha les	Kas hmi ri	Mar ath i	Guj ara ti	Pan jab ST	Lah nda	Hin di	Ben gal i	Nep ali Lst	Kha sku ra

PART 3,4

		4.1.1. Greek ML	4.1.2. Greek MD	4.1.3. Greek Mod	4.1.4. Greek D	4.2. Greek K	5.1. Armeni Mod	5.2. Armeni Lst	6.1. Osseti c	6.2.1.1. Afghan	6.2.1.2. Waziri	6.2.2.1.1. Persia Lst	6.2.2.1.2. Tadzik	6.2.2.2. Baluchi	6.2.2.3. Wakhi	7.1.1.1. Albani T	7.1.1.2. Albani Top	7.1.2. Albani G	7.2. Albani K	7.3. Albani C
2.3.2.1.	Slovenian	170	188	179	181	203	141	144	133	114	113	151	157	141	128	141	140	164	129	136
2.3.2.2.1.1.	Lusatian L	154	178	168	160	177	151	139	135	130	119	168	180	148	133	141	144	153	133	140
2.3.2.2.1.2.	Lusatian U	154	178	168	160	177	151	139	135	130	119	168	180	148	133	141	150	164	138	151
2.3.2.2.2.1.1.	Czech	149	173	164	161	177	159	151	136	126	121	153	169	138	135	130	135	148	130	142
2.3.2.2.2.1.2.	Slovak	155	178	168	171	182	153	151	136	131	115	158	174	147	140	136	141	155	130	142
2.3.2.2.2.2.	Czech E	144	162	158	161	167	153	151	128	126	120	147	163	141	128	136	140	155	131	138
2.3.2.2.3.1.	Ukrainian	149	162	158	161	167	156	150	124	120	120	147	168	141	139	131	135	148	124	130
2.3.2.2.3.2.	Byelorussian	160	178	174	176	182	153	151	130	126	120	142	158	141	139	126	130	144	124	131
2.3.2.2.4.	Polish	155	178	163	171	182	151	150	140	119	124	151	162	135	133	130	129	154	118	130
2.3.2.2.5.	Russian	159	177	168	170	181	147	141	133	120	118	156	172	146	133	141	139	164	128	141
2.3.2.2.6.1.	Macedonian	182	207	201	189	200	152	145	140	130	125	164	180	147	140	157	166	188	157	160
2.3.2.2.6.2.	Bulgarian	169	193	189	171	187	131	124	134	119	114	147	163	136	135	139	144	158	139	142
2.3.2.2.6.3.	Serbocroatian	170	188	179	182	188	141	134	134	130	120	158	174	147	145	141	145	160	135	142
3.1.	Gypsy Gk	100	97	100	96	107	91	81	123	96	98	147	161	143	117	91	90	95	90	92
3.2.	Singhalese	108	116	108	108	124	106	102	133	94	100	138	151	148	106	94	93	98	93	93
3.3.1.	Kashmiri	119	133	124	125	141	132	132	166	144	160	181	217	218	129	109	113	117	112	112
3.3.2.1.1.1.	Marathi	121	129	131	122	142	119	111	148	130	118	166	187	195	145	124	128	124	122	128
3.3.2.1.1.2.	Gujarati	94	105	104	94	104	112	104	131	133	131	143	159	192	120	102	106	101	100	105
3.3.2.1.2.1.1.	Panjabi ST	112	125	122	118	138	131	124	162	150	150	202	225	254	161	105	109	109	113	114
3.3.2.1.2.1.2.	Lahnda	118	130	127	124	144	125	118	162	158	155	216	243	251	173	104	108	109	107	113
3.3.2.1.2.2.	Hindi	117	124	126	118	133	124	117	156	153	154	185	212	240	153	108	112	108	107	112
3.3.2.1.3.	Bengali	107	120	117	119	133	115	108	156	133	148	188	204	237	147	109	113	109	108	114
3.3.2.2.1.	Nepali List	127	135	136	128	138	130	128	144	148	153	174	195	225	142	115	119	119	117	124
3.3.2.2.2.	Khaskura	136	138	141	137	141	128	125	112	124	129	143	166	190	113	106	110	109	109	108

Greek ML | Greek MD | Greek Mod | Greek D | Greek K | Armeni Mod | Armeni Lst | Osseti c | Afghan | Waziri | Persia Lst | Tadzik | Baluchi | Wakhi | Albani T | Albani Top | Albani G | Albani K | Albani C

PART 4,1

		1.1.1.	1.1.2.	1.2.1.1.	1.2.1.2.	1.2.2.1.	1.2.2.2.	1.2.2.3.	2.1.1.1.	2.1.1.2.	2.1.2.1.	2.1.2.2.	2.1.2.3.1.	2.1.2.3.2.	2.1.2.3.3.	2.1.2.4.1.	2.1.2.4.2.	2.1.2.5.	2.1.2.6.1.	2.1.2.6.2.	2.1.2.7.1.	2.1.2.7.2.1.	2.1.2.7.2.2.	2.1.2.8.
		Iri sh A	Iri sh B	Wel sh N	Wel sh C	Bre ton Lst	Bre ton SE	Bre ton ST	Rum ani Lst	Vla ch	Ita lia n	Lad in	Pro ven cal	Fre nch	Wal loo n	Fr. Cre C	Fr. Cre D	Sar din N	Sar din L	Sar din C	Spa nis h	Por tug ST	Bra zil ian	Cat ala n
4.1.1.	Greek ML	133	131	124	128	134	129	130	147	178	168	149	157	147	147	117	119	144	157	153	157	157	154	149
4.1.2.	Greek MD	151	150	137	141	147	141	142	150	177	177	152	166	155	155	125	127	147	166	156	166	161	162	153
4.1.3.	Greek Mod	142	141	133	138	144	138	139	157	183	178	158	167	157	157	122	124	153	172	157	167	167	163	154
4.1.4.	Greek D	144	142	135	140	146	141	141	154	180	174	156	163	153	153	124	126	151	165	161	163	163	160	150
4.2.	Greek K	159	159	155	160	166	160	166	168	191	190	165	179	168	168	138	141	165	184	174	173	173	170	166
5.1.	Armenian Mod	120	122	126	131	126	126	126	136	149	152	137	146	146	146	120	122	132	135	136	145	146	147	147
5.2.	Armenian List	112	109	113	118	112	112	112	118	129	138	124	133	133	133	112	114	119	122	124	132	134	134	134
6.1.	Ossetic	111	103	101	106	102	112	118	138	139	143	144	143	143	148	99	101	133	131	132	144	148	145	144
6.2.1.1.	Afghan	93	105	93	92	98	103	104	94	103	120	115	119	119	119	83	85	99	108	98	113	119	120	120
6.2.1.2.	Waziri	91	93	82	87	92	97	98	98	107	114	105	114	114	114	76	77	99	103	98	108	114	115	115
6.2.2.1.1.	Persian List	104	112	101	105	105	116	116	136	149	141	147	141	141	141	105	106	126	130	125	140	146	142	142
6.2.2.1.2.	Tadzik	120	129	116	121	121	126	127	137	157	157	153	151	151	156	111	112	137	145	131	145	151	147	147
6.2.2.2.	Baluchi	100	109	96	101	100	111	111	132	138	136	138	141	141	135	110	112	126	130	132	141	146	142	142
6.2.2.3.	Wakhi	82	90	100	105	105	118	118	149	150	140	141	140	139	145	122	123	135	139	129	134	140	140	140
7.1.1.1.	Albanian T	95	98	94	94	105	109	109	109	119	115	110	114	114	114	83	85	111	120	110	108	109	115	110
7.1.1.2.	Albanian Top	99	107	98	98	108	113	114	113	124	123	119	122	122	122	88	89	120	129	114	117	117	124	113
7.1.2.	Albanian G	104	106	99	98	110	114	115	115	124	120	110	119	120	119	88	89	117	126	122	114	114	121	115
7.2.	Albanian K	98	101	94	94	104	109	110	113	124	122	113	122	122	122	88	89	119	128	108	111	117	118	118
7.3.	Albanian C	109	111	104	104	115	120	121	125	129	134	130	134	134	134	98	99	131	141	125	128	134	135	130
		Iri sh A	Iri sh B	Wel sh N	Wel sh C	Bre ton Lst	Bre ton SE	Bre ton ST	Rum ani Lst	Vla ch	Ita lia n	Lad in	Pro ven cal	Fre nch	Wal loo n	Fr. Cre C	Fr. Cre D	Sar din N	Sar din L	Sar din C	Spa nis h	Por tug ST	Bra zil ian	Cat ala n

PART 4,2

		2.2.1.1.1.	2.2.1.1.2.	2.2.1.1.3.1.	2.2.1.1.3.2.	2.2.1.1.3.3.	2.2.1.1.4.	2.2.1.2.1.1.1.	2.2.1.2.1.1.2.	2.2.1.2.1.1.3.	2.2.1.2.1.2.	2.2.1.2.1.3.	2.2.1.2.2.1.	2.2.1.2.2.2.	2.2.2.1.	2.2.2.2.	2.3.1.1.1.	2.3.1.1.2.	2.3.1.2.
		Ger man ST	Pen Dut ch	Dut ch Lst	Afr ika ans	Fle mis h	Fri sia n	Swe dis Up	Swe dis VL	Swe dis Lst	Dan ish	Rik sma l	Ice lan ST	Far oes e	Eng lis ST	Tak ita ki	Lit hua O	Lit hua ST	Lat via n
4.1.1.	Greek ML	173	163	173	162	163	159	168	168	168	168	164	182	180	147	115	154	158	149
4.1.2.	Greek MD	188	177	194	177	190	174	188	177	184	182	179	198	189	166	134	167	182	162
4.1.3.	Greek Mod	188	179	188	172	179	175	183	178	184	183	179	198	190	162	130	162	172	152
4.1.4.	Greek D	179	169	184	173	175	166	168	174	174	179	170	194	192	158	127	160	169	149
4.2.	Greek K	210	202	215	204	207	198	205	200	206	200	192	216	207	194	153	191	205	180
5.1.	Armenian Mod	146	146	146	140	141	146	156	152	157	151	136	160	163	130	117	152	152	131
5.2.	Armenian List	128	134	139	138	139	133	144	144	149	144	129	148	157	133	114	150	154	138
6.1.	Ossetic	149	145	149	154	150	124	148	148	148	142	132	140	139	142	108	132	133	128
6.2.1.1.	Afghan	104	109	104	104	105	97	93	93	94	98	94	101	95	93	74	115	120	103
6.2.1.2.	Waziri	109	114	103	103	104	101	98	97	97	103	98	106	100	98	77	120	114	103
6.2.2.1.1.	Persian List	140	135	146	145	147	114	135	135	135	140	126	138	132	140	101	161	161	141
6.2.2.1.2.	Tadzik	147	142	147	146	153	131	146	146	147	151	137	151	143	147	108	161	155	141
6.2.2.2.	Baluchi	142	142	142	135	132	115	130	131	130	141	126	145	138	126	113	136	130	109
6.2.2.3.	Wakhi	134	127	140	133	129	114	133	134	133	127	129	132	130	123	114	110	109	121
7.1.1.1.	Albanian T	126	109	111	110	116	120	104	120	120	121	111	108	106	113	86	137	141	124
7.1.1.2.	Albanian Top	130	114	109	109	115	118	103	119	119	125	110	107	105	117	90	141	144	133
7.1.2.	Albanian G	131	119	116	116	122	125	114	124	125	131	122	118	116	129	95	142	147	135
7.2.	Albanian K	129	114	113	113	120	124	108	118	124	130	109	106	105	122	96	130	133	122
7.3.	Albanian C	130	113	114	114	121	125	114	130	130	130	120	117	115	118	90	137	135	129
		Ger man ST	Pen Dut ch	Dut ch Lst	Afr ika ans	Fle mis h	Fri sia n	Swe dis Up	Swe dis VL	Swe dis Lst	Dan ish	Rik sma l	Ice lan ST	Far oes e	Eng lis ST	Tak ita ki	Lit hua O	Lit hua ST	Lat via n

PART 4,3

		Slo ven ian	Lus ati L	Lus ati U	Cze ch	Slo vak	Cze ch E	Ukr ain ian	Bye lor uss	Pol ish	Rus sia n	Mac edo nia	Bul gar ian	Ser boc roa	Gyp sy Gk	Sin gha les	Kas hmi ri	Mar ath i	Guj ara ti	Pan jab ST	Lah nda	Hin di	Ben gal i	Nep ali Lst	Kha sku ra
		2.3.2.1.	2.3.2.2.1.1.	2.3.2.2.1.2.	2.3.2.2.2.1.1.	2.3.2.2.2.1.2.	2.3.2.2.2.2.	2.3.2.2.3.1.	2.3.2.2.3.2.	2.3.2.2.4.	2.3.2.2.5.	2.3.2.2.6.1.	2.3.2.2.6.2.	2.3.2.2.6.3.	3.1.	3.2.	3.3.1.	3.3.2.1.1.1.	3.3.2.1.1.2.	3.3.2.1.2.1.1.	3.3.2.1.2.1.2.	3.3.2.1.2.2.	3.3.2.1.3.	3.3.2.2.1.	3.3.2.2.2.
4.1.1.	Greek ML	170	154	154	149	155	144	149	160	155	159	182	169	170	100	108	119	121	94	112	118	117	107	127	136
4.1.2.	Greek MD	188	178	178	173	178	162	162	178	178	177	207	193	188	97	116	133	129	105	125	130	124	120	135	138
4.1.3.	Greek Mod	179	168	168	164	168	158	158	174	163	168	201	189	179	100	108	124	131	104	122	127	126	117	136	141
4.1.4.	Greek D	181	160	160	161	171	161	161	176	171	170	189	171	182	96	108	125	122	94	118	124	118	119	128	137
4.2.	Greek K	203	177	177	177	182	167	167	182	182	181	200	187	188	107	124	141	142	104	138	144	133	133	138	141
5.1.	Armenian Mod	141	151	151	159	153	153	156	153	151	147	152	131	141	91	106	132	119	112	131	125	124	115	130	128
5.2.	Armenian List	144	139	139	151	151	151	150	151	150	141	145	124	134	81	102	132	111	104	124	118	117	108	128	125
6.1.	Ossetic	133	135	135	136	136	128	124	130	140	133	140	134	134	123	133	166	148	131	162	162	156	156	144	112
6.2.1.1.	Afghan	114	130	130	126	131	126	120	126	119	120	130	119	130	96	94	144	130	133	150	158	153	133	148	124
6.2.1.2.	Waziri	113	119	119	121	115	120	120	120	124	118	125	114	120	98	100	160	118	131	150	155	154	148	153	129
6.2.2.1.1.	Persian List	151	168	168	153	158	147	147	142	151	156	164	147	158	147	138	181	166	143	202	216	185	188	174	143
6.2.2.1.2.	Tadzik	157	180	180	169	174	163	168	158	162	172	180	163	174	161	151	217	187	159	225	243	212	204	195	166
6.2.2.2.	Baluchi	141	148	148	138	147	141	141	141	135	146	147	136	147	143	148	218	195	192	254	251	240	237	225	190
6.2.2.3.	Wakhi	128	133	133	135	140	128	139	139	133	133	140	135	145	117	106	129	145	120	161	173	153	147	142	113
7.1.1.1.	Albanian T	141	141	141	130	136	136	131	126	130	141	157	139	141	91	94	109	124	102	105	104	108	109	115	106
7.1.1.2.	Albanian Top	140	144	150	135	141	140	135	130	129	139	166	144	145	90	93	113	128	106	109	108	112	113	119	110
7.1.2.	Albanian G	164	153	164	148	155	155	148	144	154	164	188	158	160	95	98	117	124	101	109	109	108	109	119	109
7.2.	Albanian K	129	133	138	130	130	131	124	124	118	128	157	139	135	90	93	112	122	100	113	107	107	108	117	109
7.3.	Albanian C	136	140	151	142	142	138	130	131	130	141	160	142	142	92	93	112	128	105	114	113	112	114	124	108
		Slo ven ian	Lus ati L	Lus ati U	Cze ch	Slo vak	Cze ch E	Ukr ain ian	Bye lor uss	Pol ish	Rus sia n	Mac edo nia	Bul gar ian	Ser boc roa	Gyp sy Gk	Sin gha les	Kas hmi ri	Mar ath i	Guj ara ti	Pan jab ST	Lah nda	Hin di	Ben gal i	Nep ali Lst	Kha sku ra

PART 4,4

		4.1.1. Greek ML	4.1.2. Greek MD	4.1.3. Greek Mod	4.1.4. Greek D	4.2. Greek K	5.1. Armeni Mod	5.2. Armeni Lst	6.1. Ossetic	6.2.1.1. Afghan	6.2.1.2. Waziri	6.2.2.1.1. Persia Lst	6.2.2.1.2. Tadzik	6.2.2.2. Baluchi	6.2.2.3. Wakhi	7.1.1.1. Albani T	7.1.1.2. Albani Top	7.1.2. Albani G	7.2. Albani K	7.3. Albani C
4.1.1.	Greek ML	0	923	869	893	673	182	149	99	83	92	126	132	122	99	104	103	109	103	102
4.1.2.	Greek MD	923	0	918	907	696	190	162	112	90	94	138	138	124	101	117	116	122	115	114
4.1.3.	Greek Mod	869	918	0	868	675	187	154	99	88	93	125	135	122	99	113	117	118	117	118
4.1.4.	Greek D	893	907	868	0	750	178	161	104	89	93	126	127	122	94	111	109	115	109	109
4.2.	Greek K	673	696	675	750	0	188	172	143	94	99	142	148	128	111	130	129	137	128	135
5.1.	Armenian Mod	182	190	187	178	188	0	722	103	90	106	128	144	140	102	80	79	83	84	88
5.2.	Armenian List	149	162	154	161	172	722	0	99	87	96	115	126	120	85	82	81	85	86	90
6.1.	Ossetic	99	112	99	104	143	103	99	0	170	185	266	277	229	234	89	88	93	88	99
6.2.1.1.	Afghan	83	90	88	89	94	90	87	170	0	749	308	355	286	263	68	73	71	73	77
6.2.1.2.	Waziri	92	94	93	93	99	106	96	185	749	0	269	289	269	210	71	71	73	71	74
6.2.2.1.1.	Persian List	126	138	125	126	142	128	115	266	308	269	0	815	443	402	96	96	99	90	99
6.2.2.1.2.	Tadzik	132	138	135	127	148	144	126	277	355	289	815	0	462	442	102	106	107	101	111
6.2.2.2.	Baluchi	122	124	122	122	128	140	120	229	286	269	443	462	0	352	92	91	94	90	94
6.2.2.3.	Wakhi	99	101	99	94	111	102	85	234	263	210	402	442	352	0	89	94	93	94	104
7.1.1.1.	Albanian T	104	117	113	111	130	80	82	89	68	71	96	102	92	89	0	879	840	736	706
7.1.1.2.	Albanian Top	103	116	117	109	129	79	81	88	73	71	96	106	91	94	879	0	800	734	722
7.1.2.	Albanian G	109	122	118	115	137	83	85	93	71	73	99	107	94	93	840	800	0	707	706
7.2.	Albanian K	103	115	117	109	128	84	86	88	73	71	90	101	90	94	736	734	707	0	704
7.3.	Albanian C	102	114	118	109	135	88	90	99	77	74	99	111	94	104	706	722	706	704	0

Greek ML | Greek MD | Greek Mod | Greek D | Greek K | Armeni Mod | Armeni Lst | Ossetic | Afghan | Waziri | Persia Lst | Tadzik | Baluchi | Wakhi | Albani T | Albani Top | Albani G | Albani K | Albani C

A6. THE PAIR-GROUP METHOD OF CLUSTERING

The pair-group clustering method is an iterative procedure based on a simple conception. It uses a square matrix (i.e., table) of similarities between all the speech varieties. The matrix is assumed to be symmetric, i.e., the value in row i and column j = the value in row j and column i for all i and j. In each iteration, the following steps are done:

(1) The largest similarity in the matrix is found.

(2) The two speech varieties and/or groups which it connects, call them X and Y, are joined to form a new group, call it N.

(3) The rows and columns corresponding to X and Y are removed from the matrix.

(4) A new row and column corresponding to N is added to the matrix.

Note that these steps reduce the number of speech varieties and/or groups by one (and also the size of the matrix by one). This iteration is repeated until only one group is left. Of course, step (4) requires a method for calculating the similarities in the new row and column. The pair-group method has different versions according to how this is done.

The "single-linkage" version uses the minimum of all the similarities between ultimate members of X and ultimate members of Y. The "complete-linkage" version uses the maximum of these similarities. The "averaging" version uses the average, possibly weighted, of these similarities, and comes in two main varieties, UPGMA and WPGMA, which correspond to two different weighting schemes. The acronyms come from the phrases "unweighted pair-group method agglomerative" and "weighted . . . ." Each of these weighting schemes is natural in a different context. The averaging version used here, UPGMA, gives equal weight to every ultimate similarity when averaging. This is different from the weighting scheme used for averaging in the procedure of this paper (as described in Section 2.3), which agrees with the weighting method of WPGMA. Full descriptions of all these methods may be found in Sneath and Sokal (1973) on the following pages: single-linkage version, 216-222; complete-linkage version, 222-223; UPGMA, 223-228; WPGMA, 228-235. Incidentally, the terminology of "weighted" versus "unweighted" is widely known to be confusing. The weights referred to are only implicit, and do not pertain to the subgroups that constitute the group. Instead, they pertain to the ultimate members of the subgroups, here speech varieties. The ultimate members are unweighted or weighted, implicitly, in the two methods. The step that is explicitly programmed, however, uses weights or does not use weights exactly contrary to the name.

From the definitions above it is clear that the single-linkage and complete-linkage versions are opposite extremes, in that one uses the minimum similarity and the other the maximum similarity. The averaging version is intermediate, in that it uses an average similarity, which lies between them minimum and the maximum.

It can be seen from the description above that a classification formed by the pair-group method is necessarily dichotomous, i.e., every group has exactly two immediate members. It is widely realized that not every group need be meaningful, and that in some cases a group should be dissolved, i.e., its immediate members should be made into immediate members of the next higher group. However, it is widely believed that the method for deciding which groups should be dissolved depends on the subject matter in which the subgrouping is being done. All the generally accepted methods for making this decision use additional assumptions that are peculiar to one or another area of application.

A7. THE PROBABILITY THAT $p_1 - p_2 \geq 0.08$

This appendix is intended to be read in connection with the description of the subgrouping method in Section 2.2, and uses terminology provided there. During the subgrouping method, a nucleus N_1 is obtained with mating percentage p_1. Its critical percentage, which is shared with pool member Z, is p_2. Should N_1 and Z be mated to form a new nucleus? Originally, this decision was made on the basis of a statistical test. If $|p_1 - p_2|$ was small enough to be ascribable to chance, given that Z and the immediate members of N_1 all belong to the same group, then the mating was performed. Otherwise, it was not.

"Ascribable to chance" was identified with a probability $\geq 10\%$. Thus if $|p_1 - p_2|$ was small enough to occur with probability $\geq 10\%$, then the mating was performed. The statistical test originally used always yielded, in practice, a threshold for $|p_1 - p_2|$ close to 0.08 (8 percentage points). Thus for practicality, a threshold of 8 percentage points was substituted for the statistical test.

Now look at this matter from a slightly different viewpoint, and consider the probability that $|p_1 - p_2| \geq 0.08$. This probability was originally calculated to be 10%. This result was the original basis for choosing 8 percentage points as the criterion. This appendix first presents calculations like the original ones. Then it presents more realistic calculations which show that the relevant probability is in fact far smaller than 10%, i.e., the 8 percentage point criterion is very conservative.

To decide whether the difference can be ascribed to chance requires precise definition of the relevant event and the calculation of its probability, which in turn requires a stochastic model. In this context, statisticians call such a model the "null hypothesis". The test originally used was a chi-square test that is mathematically equivalent to the following more simply described test. Let $M = 200$ be the number of meanings. (M is also the denominator of the percentages). The null hypothesis is that p_1 and p_2 are chosen independently from the same binomial distribution with parameters p_0 and M, for some p_0. The event is that a difference as large as 0.08 or larger would be observed between p_1 and p_2, i.e., that $|p_1 - p_2| \geq 0.08$. The maximum likelihood estimate for the value of p_0 is used, namely, $p_0 = \bar{p} = (p_1 + p_2)/2$.

Recall that the expected value and the variance of the binomial distribution are p_0 and $p_0(1-p_0)/M$. Approximating the binomial distribution by a Normal distribution in the standard manner, and using the null hypothesis, $p_1 - p_2$ is Normal with mean 0 and variance $2\bar{p}(1-\bar{p})/M$. Thus the probability that $|p_1 - p_2| \geq 0.08$ is the two-tail probability that a standard Normal variable exceeds $\sqrt{0.64/\bar{p}(1-\bar{p})}$. The values of this probability for several values of $\bar{p}$ are shown in column 1 of Table 5.

The five middle values are approximately 10%, which reflects the original basis for choosing the level of 8.0 percentage points, while the top few and bottom few values in column 1 yield smaller probabilities. The pattern of larger probabilities in the middle with smaller ones above and below holds in all the columns.

Now consider the situation more closely. If N_1 and Z are mated and the resulting nucleus is called N_2, then N_2 or a larger nucleus containing it must eventually become a group, as described in Step 2 of the subgrouping method. Consider the set S of members that would be obtained from N_2 by using Step 2 on it. S must contain three or more immediate members, which are denoted by X, Y, Z, ... (Each is either a list or a group.) Now p_1 must be the percentage between a pair of members of S, while p_2 is the percentage between another such pair. Note that the two pairs may or may not share a member in common.

Then the question is whether the percentages among the members of S could reasonably lead by chance to a difference between p_1 and p_2 as large as 0.08. Denote the number of members of S by K, so that $K \geq 3$. The way in which p_1 and p_2 arise from the percentages among the members of S is somewhat complex. If $K = 3$, then there are three percentages among the members of S, with p_1 the largest and p_2 the middle one. To describe the general case, s and t are used to indicate the elements of S, and $p(s,t)$ is used to indicate the percentage between s and t, with $p(s,s) = 0$ for all s. Then consider the maximum of each of the K rows, i.e., $\max_t p(s,t)$ for each of the K values of s. Of these row maxima, it is possible to deduce that p_2 is the smallest and p_1 the second smallest.

There are several improvements in realism that are desirable in the test just used. Five of them are listed below and numbered. It turns out that each one of them tends to make the true significance levels more stringent, i.e., to make the cited probability smaller. All the

Table 5

PROBABILITIES OF SOME CONDITIONS ON $\Delta p = p_1 - p_2$ UNDER THE NULL HYPOTHESIS

All probabilities are expressed as *percentages*. Δp means $p_1 - p_2$.
"Two-tail" refers to the probability that $|\Delta p| \geq 8\%$, "one-tail" to the probability that $\Delta p \geq 8\%$.

Two-tail or one-tail–		Two-tail	One-tail								
p_1 and p_2 are–		Inde-pendent	Independent			Dependent by pair overlap			Fully dependent, with $K = 3$		
r_m is –		const.	const.	χ^2_4	unif.	const.	χ^2_4	unif.	const.	χ^2_4	unif.
Calcul. by–		Theory	Theory			Theory			Simulation		
Col. no. is–		1	2	3	4	5	6	7	8	9	10
	10	.77	.38	.08	.02	.11	.01	.00	.0	.0	.0
	20	4.55	2.28	.97	.56	.81	.20	.09	.4	.0	.3
	30	8.09	4.04	2.20	1.75	1.49	.58	.44	.9	.2	.4
	40	10.25	5.12	3.18	2.92	1.85	.90	.84	1.1	.4	.6
$\bar{p}$	50	10.96	5.48	3.71	3.65	1.83	1.03	1.05	1.0	.4	.7
	60	10.25	5.12	3.70	3.78	1.48	.93	.98	.9	.4	.6
	70	8.09	4.04	3.07	3.20	.90	.61	.65	.5	.2	.6
	80	4.55	2.28	1.80	1.90	.30	.21	.23	.1	.0	.3
	90	.77	.38	.31	.33	.01	.01	.01	.0	.0	.0

improvements except the last one are explored numerically in Table 5. They are discussed in an order that simplifies the discussion, *not* the order of importance.

(1) Since p_1 must be greater than p_2 by construction, it would be more realistic to use the one-tail probability. Changing to the one-tail probability (and making no other changes), the probabilities are simply reduced by a factor of 2. The one-tail probabilities are displayed in column 2.

(2) Use of the binomial distribution above was based on the classical assumption of glottochronology that replacement rates r_m are the same for all 200 meanings. However, it was pointed out long ago by Lounsbury (1961), Joos (1964), and Van der Merwe (1966) that this assumption is unrealistic. (See also Appendix 3.) Using unequal values for the r_m causes the binomial distribution to be replaced by a Bernoulli-Poisson distribution which depends on the values of the r_m. Dyen, James, and Cole (1967) demonstrated empirically that the r_m differ substantially, and Kruskal, Dyen, and Black (1973) investigated the r_m values in some detail for three different language families. Based on empirical evidence in the latter paper, two distributions were chosen here as providing different reasonable approximations to the distribution of the r_m values, namely, a uniform distribution from 0 to a certain upper limit and a certain scaled χ_4^2 distribution.

Columns 3 and 4 show the single-tail probabilities based on these two distributions. (The theoretical calculation leading to these two columns used Normal approximations to the resulting Bernoulli-Poisson distributions in the same manner that Normal approximations to the Bernoulli distribution were used above.) These columns have probabilities considerably below those based on the classical assumption. Furthermore, the probabilities are similar in the two columns, suggesting that the exact distribution assumed for the r_m does not affect the test probabilities very much as long as the distribution has a reasonable amount of dispersion.

(3) Whenever the pairs for p_1 and p_2 share a member in common, their overlap introduces a strong dependence and positive correlation between the two p_k, which reduces the variance of $p_1 - p_2$ and hence reduces the numerical significance levels. Whenever S contains only three immediate members, which after two is the most common size, the two pairs *must* overlap. Columns 5, 6, 7 present results parallel to those

for columns 2, 3, 4, but with the assumption that the pairs overlap replacing the assumption that p_1 and p_2 are independent. This results in a substantial further reduction of the probabilities.

(4) Even if there is no overlap between the pairs for p_1 and the pairs for p_2, the two p_k are certainly not independent, as attested to by the fact that $p_1 \geq p_2$. The dependence introduced in this way is complex and not easy to understand. To explore this, a simulation (i.e., a Monte Carlo calculation) was used. (This is still based, as is the work above, on the Normal approximation to the Bernoulli-Poisson distribution.) Columns 8, 9, 10 in the table present the results from this simulation. (As a check, the values in columns 5, 6, 7 were also simulated. The results were compatible with the calculated values shown in the table.) This yields a further decrease in the probabilities.

(5) In many cases, the elements of S are not lists but groups. The averaging process used in forming a closed group percentage reduces its variance substantially below the binomial variance for a single list, which was used in the tests above. The maximizing process used to form an open group percentage has a subtler effect and it may not reduce the variance, but it is unlikely to increase it very much. The complex mixture of averaging and maximizing that go into forming the percentages of many groups reduces the variance to the extent that averaging is used in the mixture. The effect of this improvement was not investigated numerically.

INDEX

This index is primarily an index of topics. However, it also includes all references in the text to names of languages, speech varieties, and groups of speech varieties, all references in the text to personal names, all references in Appendix 4 to colleagues who supplied word lists, and all references in the text to specific Chapters, Sections, Appendices, Tables, and Figures.

- K -

- L -

- M -

- N -

FIGURE 1. **Box diagram of Indoeuropean.**

LEX

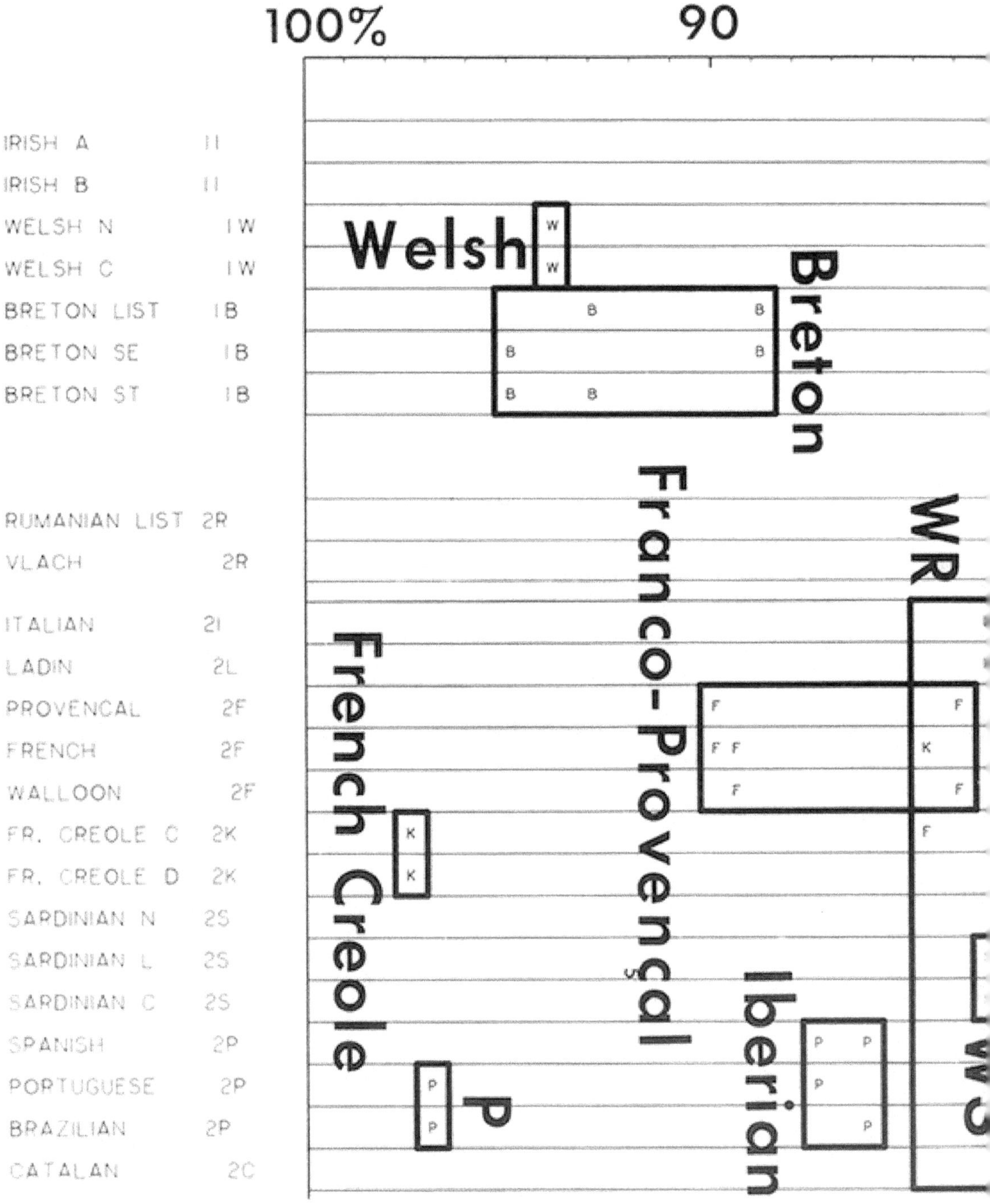

100% 90

IRISH A 1I
IRISH B 1I
WELSH N 1W
WELSH C 1W
BRETON LIST 1B
BRETON SE 1B
BRETON ST 1B

RUMANIAN LIST 2R
VLACH 2R

ITALIAN 2I
LADIN 2L
PROVENCAL 2F
FRENCH 2F
WALLOON 2F
FR. CREOLE C 2K
FR. CREOLE D 2K
SARDINIAN N 2S
SARDINIAN L 2S
SARDINIAN C 2S
SPANISH 2P
PORTUGUESE 2P
BRAZILIAN 2P
CATALAN 2C

Welsh
Breton
Franco-Provençal
French Creole
WR
Iberian
P

STATISTICAL CLASS

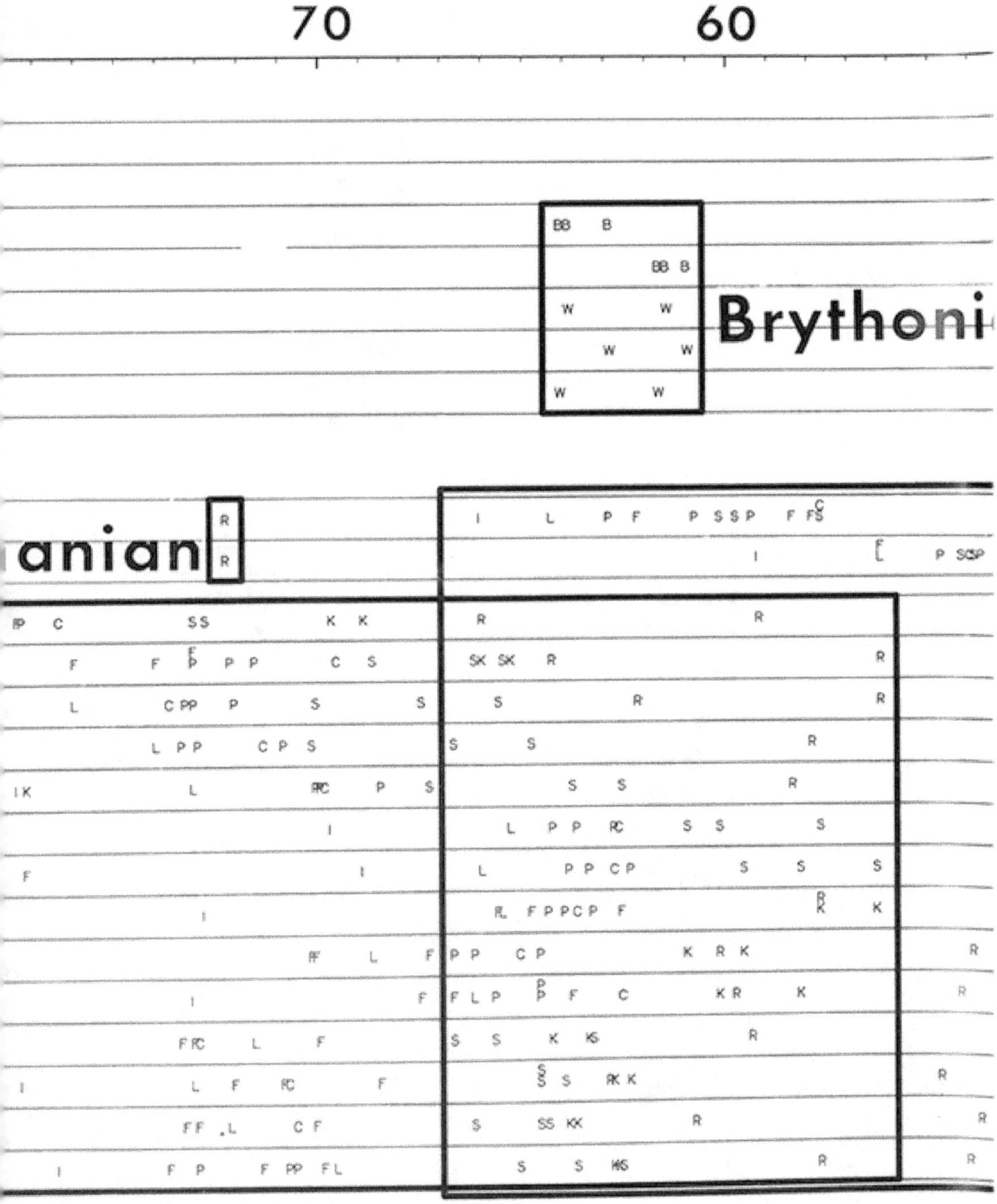

70 60

Brythoni

anian

IFICATION OF IND

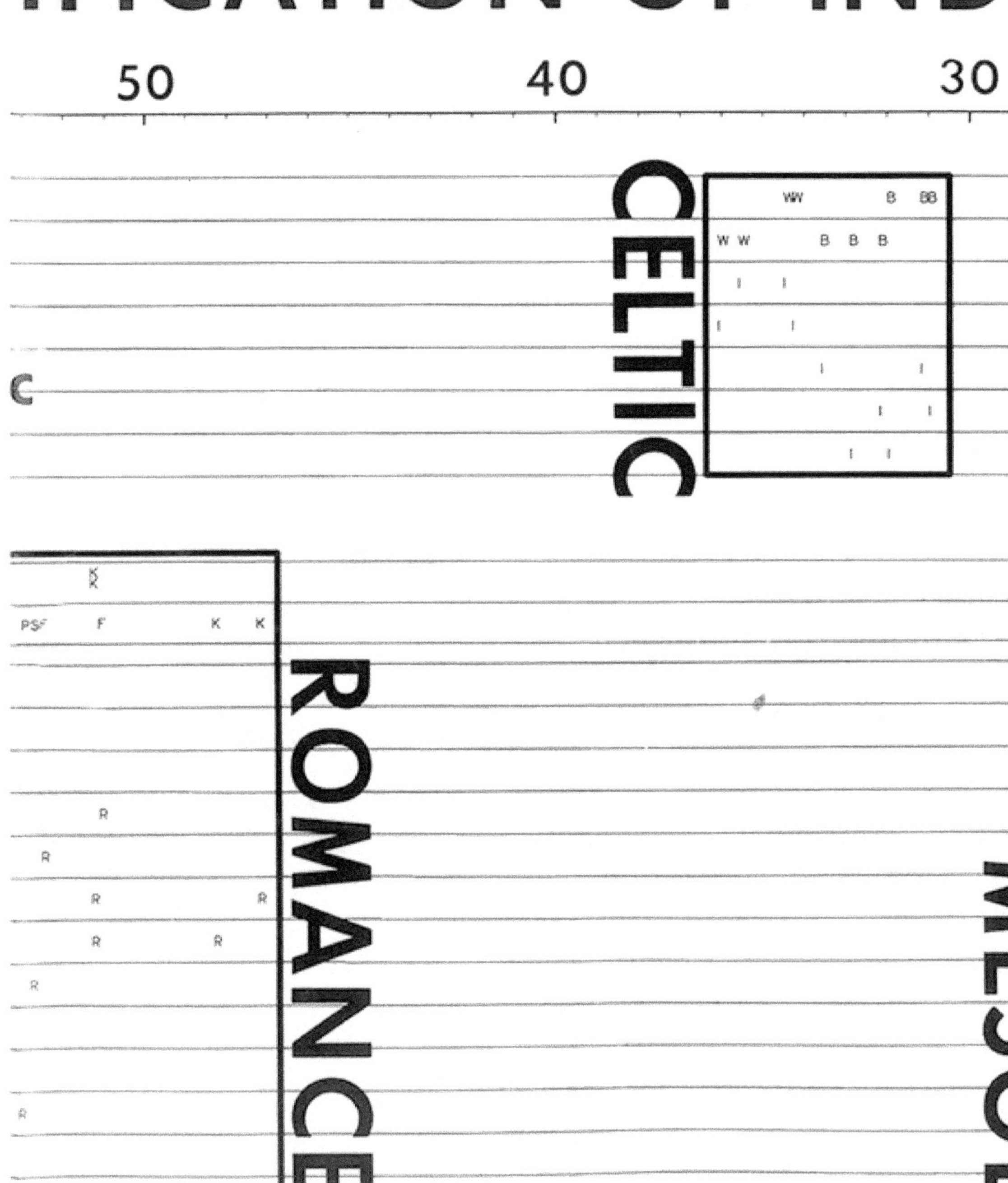

ROPEAN

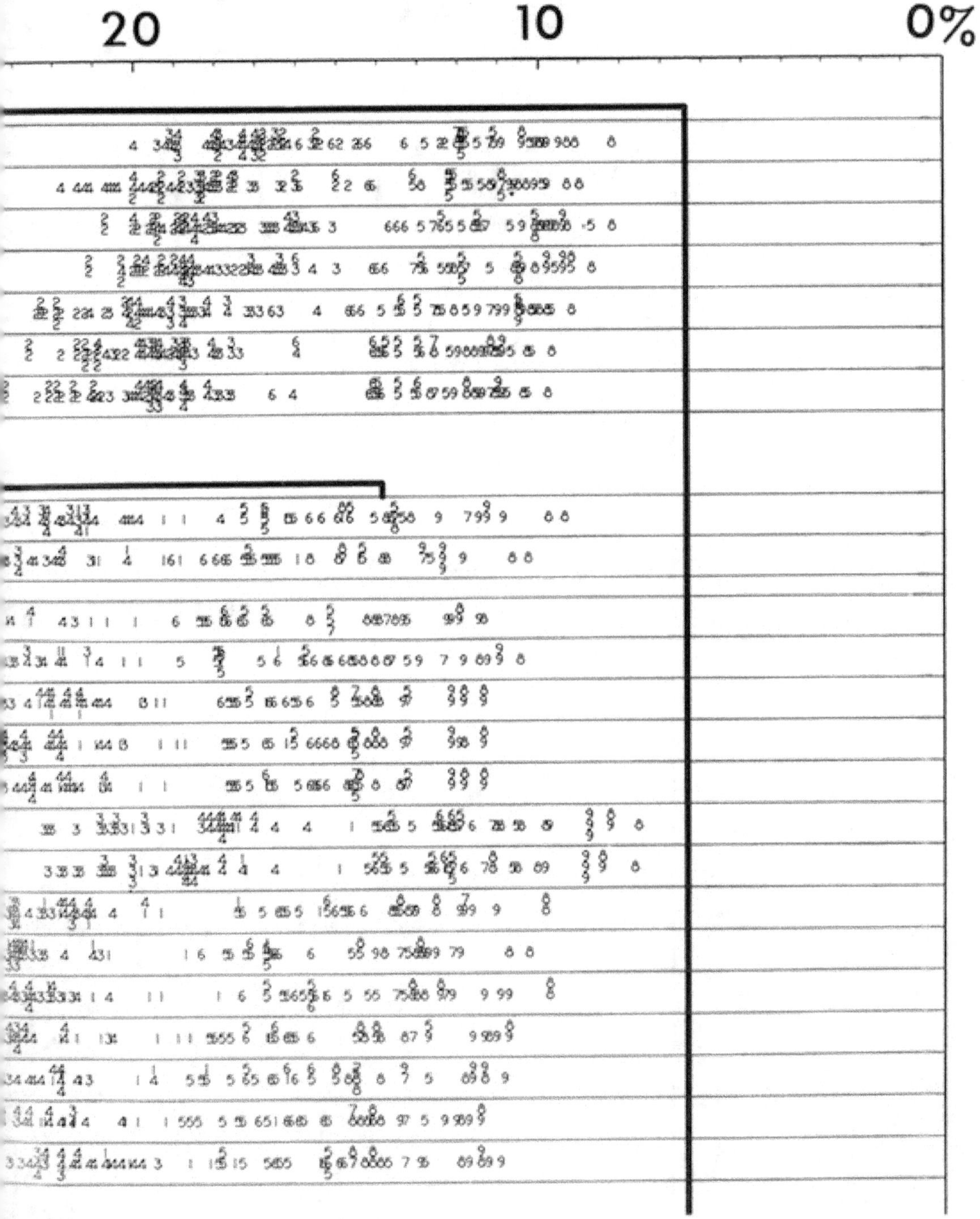

20 10 0%

GERMAN ST	3G
PENN. DUTCH	3P
DUTCH LIST	3D
FLEMISH	3D
FRISIAN	3F
SWEDISH UP	3S
SWEDISH VL	3S
SWEDISH LIST	3S
DANISH	3S
RIKSMAL	3S
ICELANDIC	3I
FAROESE	3I
ENGLISH	3E
TAKITAKI	3T
LITHUANIAN O	4B
LITHUANIAN	4B
LATVIAN	4B
SLOVENIAN	4S
LUSATIAN L	4L
LUSATIAN U	4L
CZECH	4C
SLOVAK	4C
CZECH E	4C
UKRANIAN	4U
BYELORUSSIAN	4U
POLISH	4P
RUSSIAN	4R
MACEDONIAN	4M
BULGARIAN	4M
SERBOCROATIAN	4M

Dutch-German

Dutch

Swedish

Scv

Icelandic

Lithuan

Lusatian

Czechoslov

Czechoslo

ECS

SS

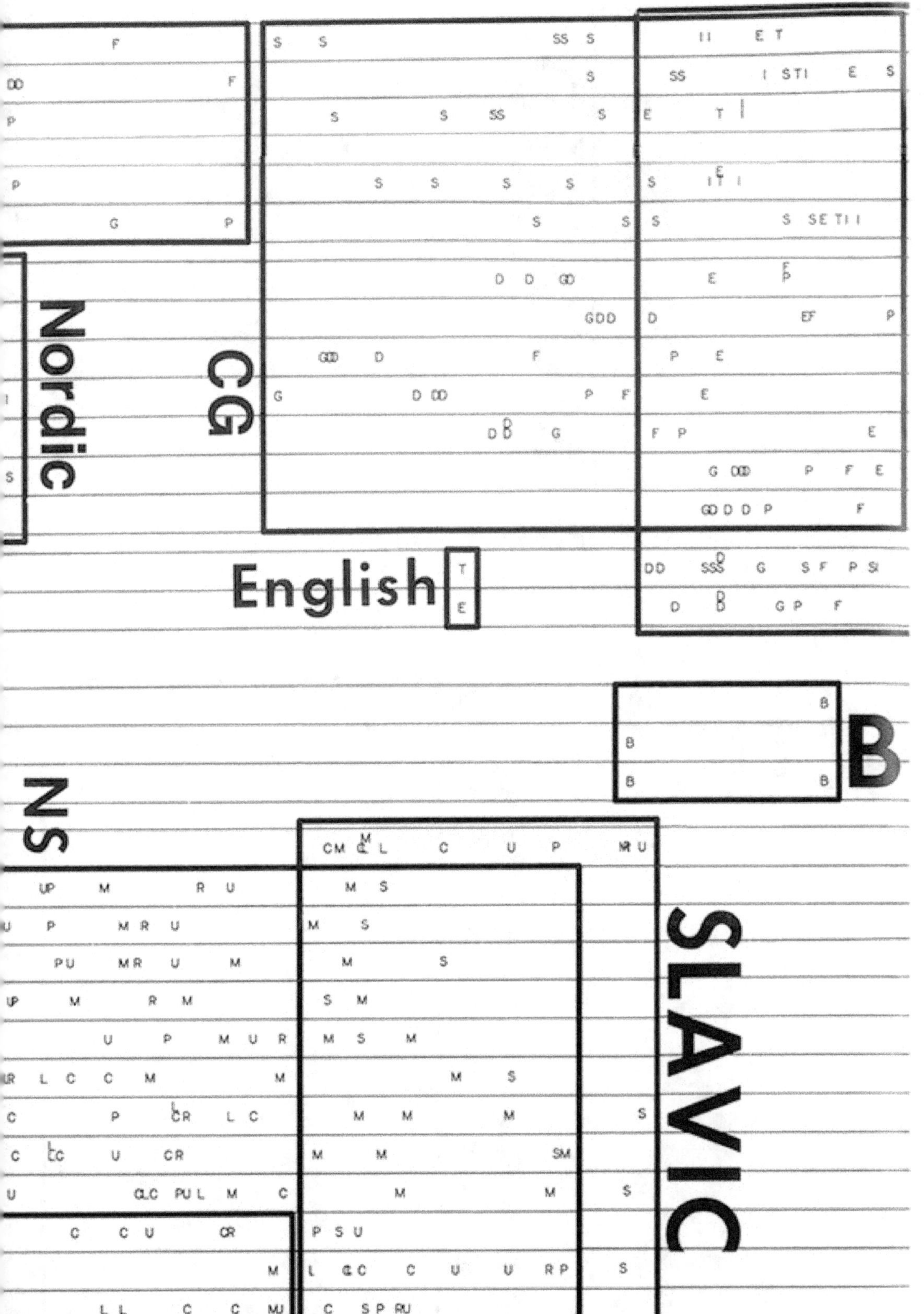

Nordic
CG
English
B
NS
SLAVIC

ALTIC

BALTOSLAVIC

ML WRC U CP MS M S
L CM RCWC PM MS
U RCML L MCP CS M
B BB
B B B
B B B
B B B
B B B
B B B
BB B
BB B
B B B
B B B
BB B
B B B
B B B

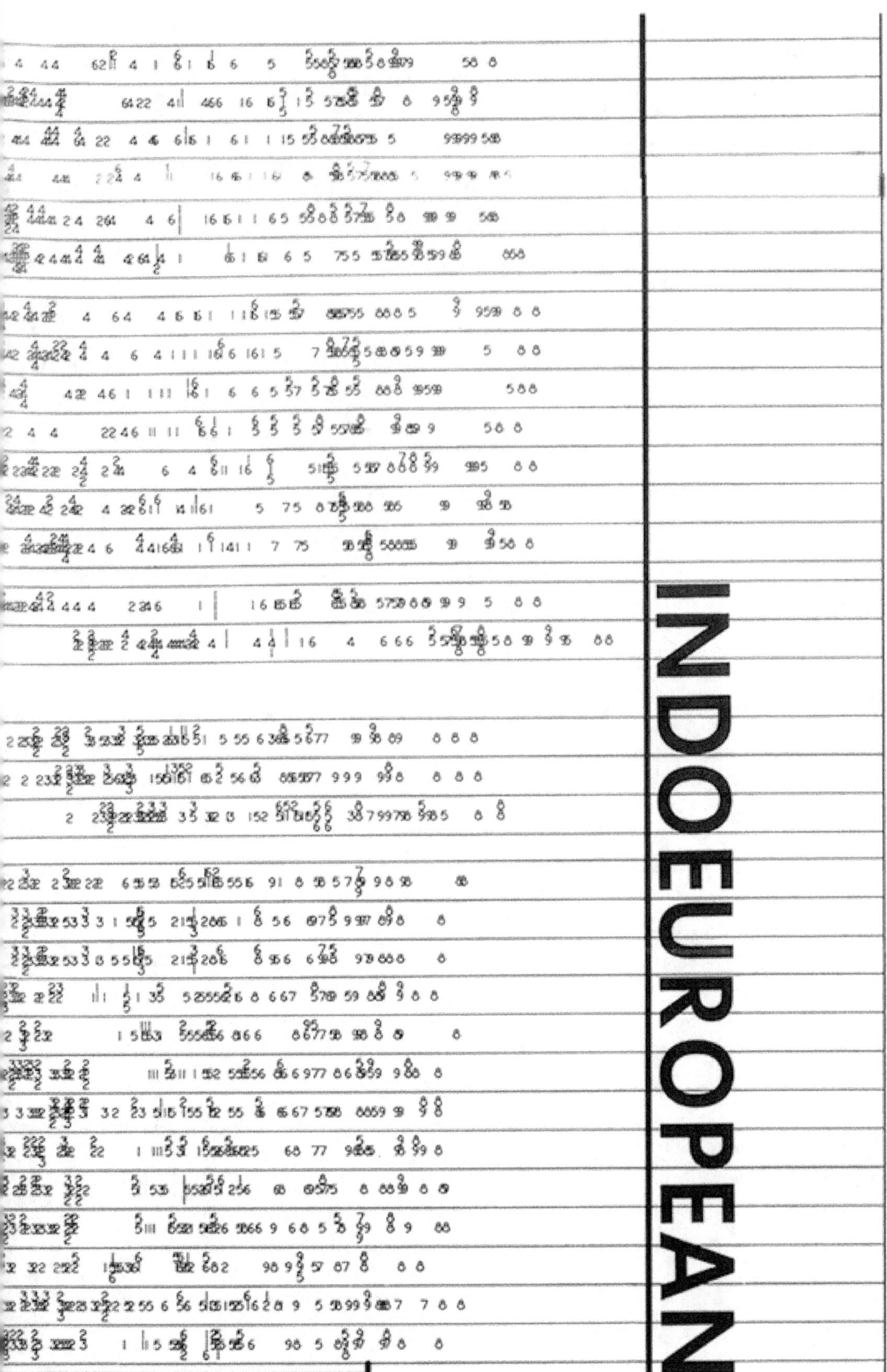
INDOEUROPEAN

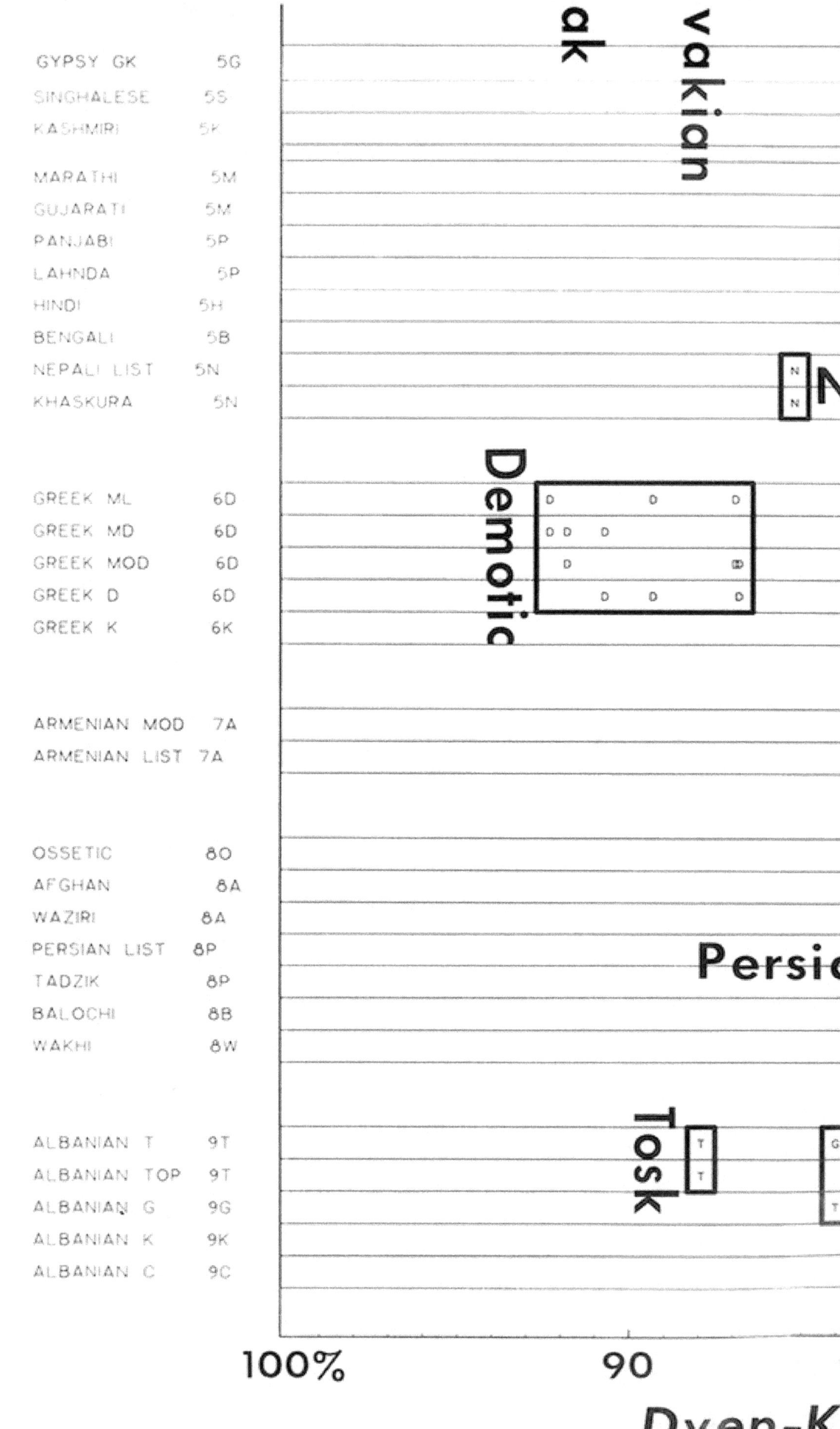

GYPSY GK 5G
SINGHALESE 5S
KASHMIRI 5K
MARATHI 5M
GUJARATI 5M
PANJABI 5P
LAHNDA 5P
HINDI 5H
BENGALI 5B
NEPALI LIST 5N
KHASKURA 5N
GREEK ML 6D
GREEK MD 6D
GREEK MOD 6D
GREEK D 6D
GREEK K 6K
ARMENIAN MOD 7A
ARMENIAN LIST 7A
OSSETIC 8O
AFGHAN 8A
WAZIRI 8A
PERSIAN LIST 8P
TADZIK 8P
BALOCHI 8B
WAKHI 8W
ALBANIAN T 9T
ALBANIAN TOP 9T
ALBANIAN G 9G
ALBANIAN K 9K
ALBANIAN C 9C
Demotic
Tosk
100%
90

Black January 1974

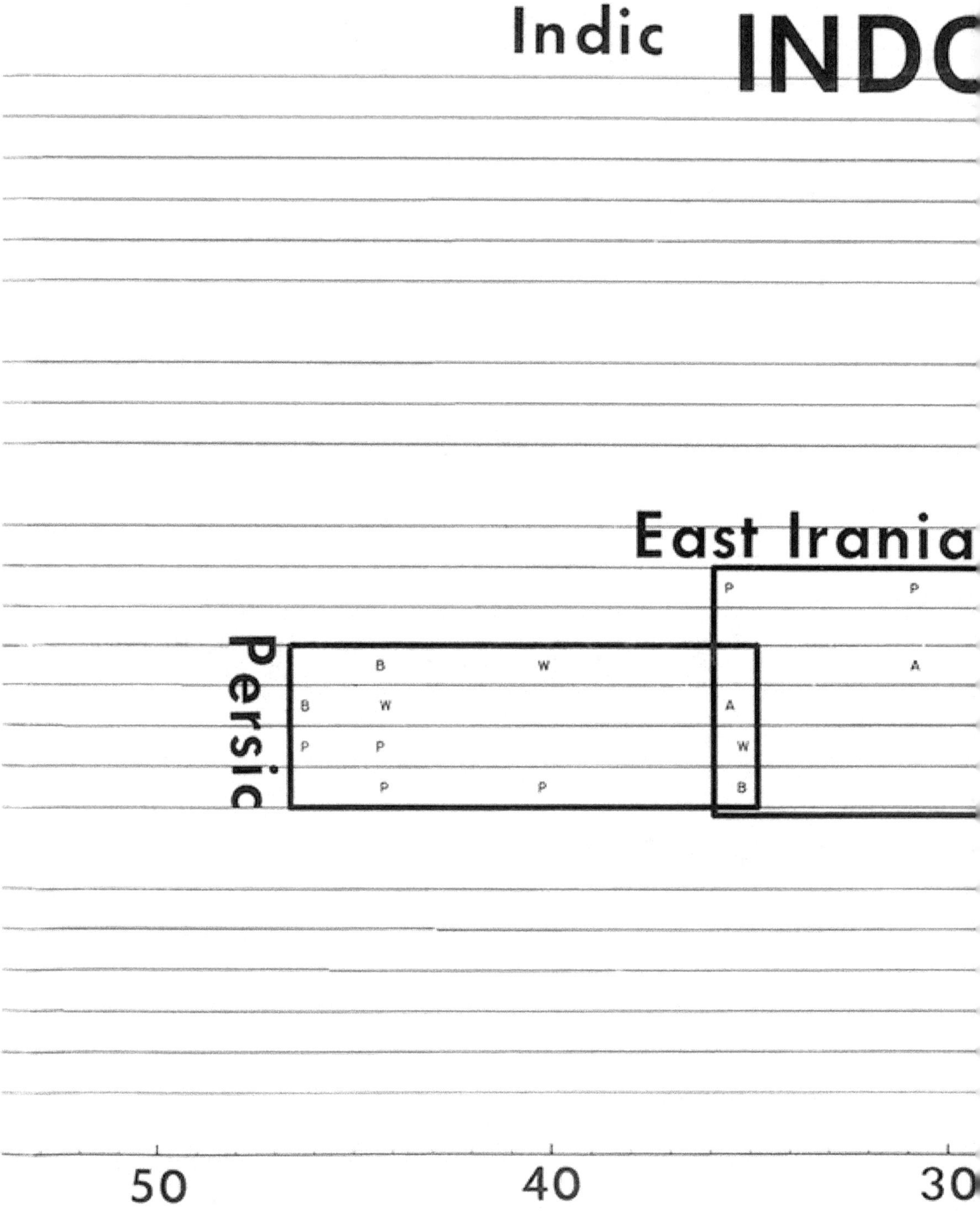

Indic INDO

East Irania

Persic

				P	P
	B	W			A
B	W			A	
P	P			W	
	P	P		B	

50 40 30

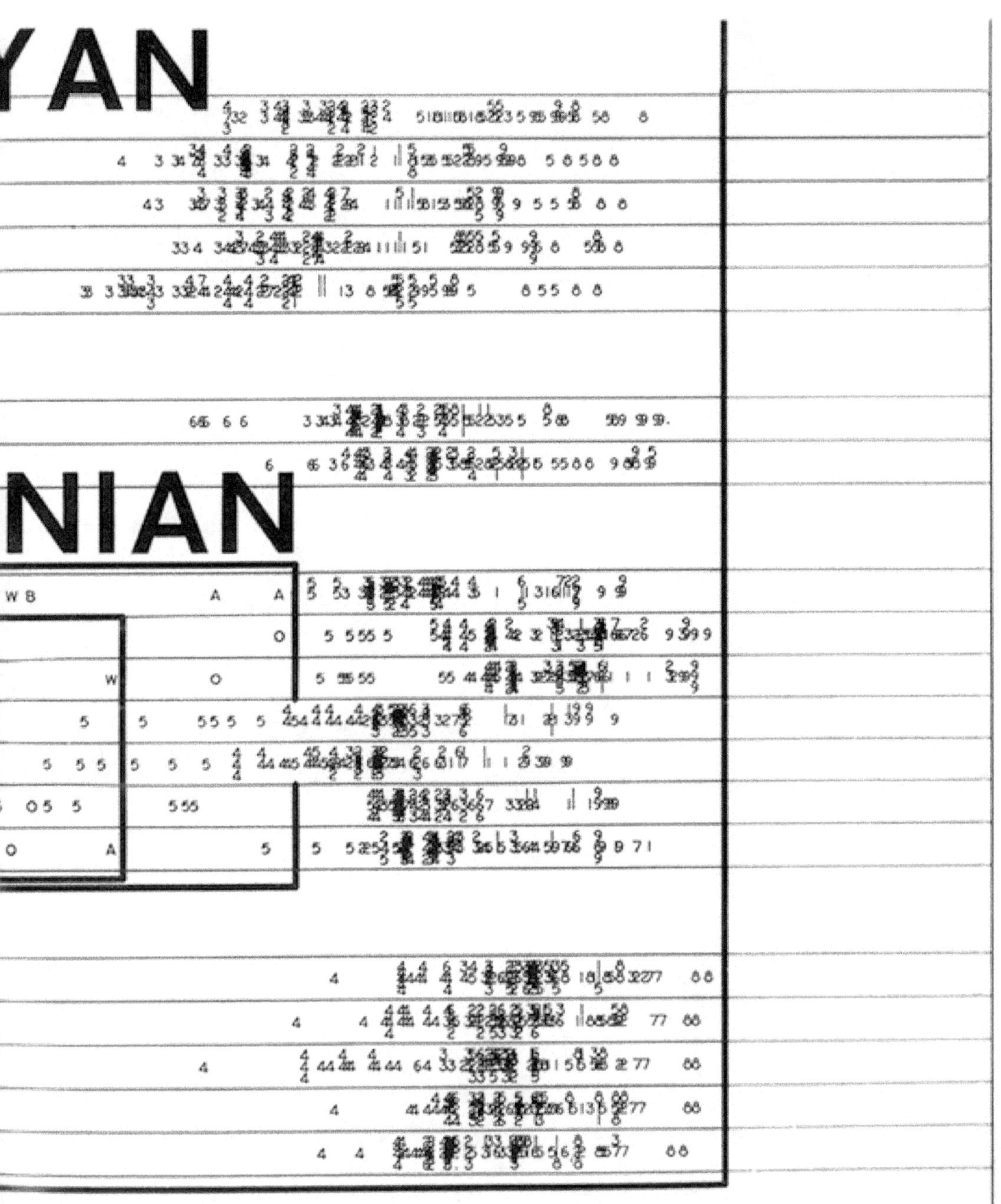
YAN
NIAN
20
10
0%

www.ingramcontent.com/pod-product-compliance
Lightning Source LLC
LaVergne TN
LVHW081602100826
845153LV00004B/444
9780871698254